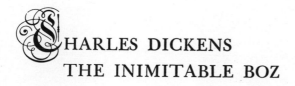
CHARLES DICKENS
THE INIMITABLE BOZ

CHARLES DICKENS:

Illustrated

Katharine E. Wilkie

THE NIMITABLE ʒOZ

Abelard-Schuman · London · New York · Toronto

an Intext *publisher*

© *Copyright 1970 by Katharine E. Wilkie*

Library of Congress Catalogue Card Number: 69-14245
Standard Book Number: 200.71598.4

LONDON	NEW YORK	TORONTO
Abelard-Schuman	*Abelard-Schuman*	*Abelard-Schuman*
Limited	*Limited*	*Canada Limited*
8 King Street	*257 Park Ave. S.*	*200 Yorkland Blvd.*
WC2	*10010*	*425*

Printed in the United States of America
Designed by The Etheredges

To My Class of 1966–1967
Who read DAVID COPPERFIELD
and
Our Student Teachers
Susan Masters
and
Susan Mayer

ONTENTS

ILLUSTRATIONS

CKNOWLEDGMENTS

Grateful acknowledgment is made to Little, Brown and Company for use of the pictures on pages 16, 22, 31, 34, 47, 49, 81, 91, 96, 99, 108, 115, 123, 128, 129, 132, 143, 150, 154, 157, 171, 172, 175, 177; to Dickens House for the pictures on pages 59, 66, 83, 103, 165; and to the New York Public Library for the picture on page 20.

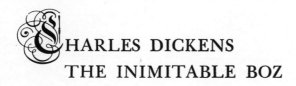

CHARLES DICKENS
THE INIMITABLE BOZ

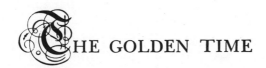

THE GOLDEN TIME

The imposing brick house at 2 Ordnance Terrace in Chatham was flooded with lights from the top floor to the bottom. John Dickens and his wife Elizabeth were entertaining again. For the household of a clerk in the Navy Pay Office, the couple did considerable party-giving.

No one was enjoying the last-minute preparations more than young Charles Dickens. The eight-year-old boy looked forward to these festive occasions when lovely ladies and elegant gentlemen filled the house with their voices and laughter. At such times he eyed his sparkling, dynamic father with adoration. He even thought his mother, in spite of her receding chin, slightly pretty.

Tonight the boy was wearing his best clothes. He carried himself proudly. With his light, curly hair, bright-blue eyes and sensitive features, he looked for all the world like an actor waiting in the wings to be called on stage.

His sister Fanny, older by two years, must have thought so, too. She had come up behind him and playfully clasped her hands over his eyes.

"Guess who?"

Charles brushed away her hands impatiently. "Oh, it's you, Fan."

"My, aren't we touchy!" she exclaimed. "What will you sing for the guests tonight, little brother?"

Sudden tears sprang to his eyes. He loved Fanny dearly. Perhaps that was why her teasing wounded him. But then, anything was likely to wound Charles—or cause him the greatest delight. For him there were no halfway stages.

"Come, my little Tom Thumb, you aren't going to cry, are you?" Her voice was warm in spite of her careless manner.

"Of course not," Charles returned, winking back the tears. He looked at her anxiously. "You *do* think Father will let me sing, don't you?"

Fanny laughed lightly. "He will have us both warbling away like nightingales. Especially you. You are his golden boy, you know. You are just like him."

"How am I like him?" Charles demanded.

She reflected for a moment. "As though you didn't know. You both love gaiety, conversation, and—and gracious living."

"Like tonight?"

She nodded. "Like tonight. You both adore being the

center of attention and generally are. And you can both talk your way out of anything."

Charles's cheeks reddened. "I'm not sure I like that description."

Fanny gave him a sisterly hug. "It fits you. I think you are adorable, and I wouldn't change you a bit even if I could."

The boy felt his heart grow warm. He was quick to respond to praise and affection. Suddenly he found himself overjoyed to be a part of the family at 2 Ordnance Terrace. Besides Father, Mother and darling Fan, there were Letitia, aged four, and baby Frederick. And there was Aunt Fanny, Mother's widowed sister, who had recently come to live with them. And, he mustn't forget Mary Weller, their maid of all work and Charles's friend, who told delightfully horrible tales of murderers and their victims. "Tales to make one's flesh creep," Charles told himself with a pleasurable shiver. Yes, Ordnance Terrace was a good place for a boy to live in 1820.

There was the sound of wheels outside. The first carriage had arrived. Presently there came a knock at the front door, and Mary Weller, in a stiffly starched cap and apron, hurried past him. Mother was coming down the stairs on Father's arm. In Charles's eyes they were a handsome couple. He shivered in anticipation. The party was about to begin.

The hours that followed were all that he had dreamed. His parents mingled with their guests, and the guests graciously accepted their hospitality. Young Charles basked in the sparkling atmosphere, which grew livelier as the evening progressed.

At last the moment arrived for which he had been waiting. Fanny had played the piano and received applause. She played, Charles thought, better than most grownups.

With a wave of his hand, Father stepped forward. Charles thought of the leading man in the play he had seen last

Ordnance Terrace, Chatham, Dickens' home from 1817 to 1821

Christmas in the little Theatre Royal in Chatham. Not even he had possessed more charm and magnetism than Father.

"And now, my friends, for the *pièce de résistance*," John Dickens began in his familiar rolling tones, "here is my son —my pride and joy, Charles, who—ah—will now recite for you 'The Destruction of Sennacherib,' by Lord Byron."

With a regal sweep of his arm, he reached down and lifted the boy to the top of the table beside him. Charles looked down solemnly at the sea of upturned faces, then in a boyish treble began:

> *The Assyrian came down like the wolf on the fold,*
> *And his cohorts were gleaming in purple and gold . . .*

The party did not break up until long after midnight. Charles, sent to bed after he and Fanny had followed his recitation with a comic duet, "The Cat's Meat Man," was lulled to sleep by the sound of laughter and talking that continued into the night.

He drifted off to sleep, secure in the knowledge that his performance had been favorably received. All his life Charles Dickens would thrive on such knowledge and be miserable when it was not forthcoming.

The family slept late the next morning. It was well past noon when the boy awoke, dressed himself and went downstairs to join the others. It was Sunday and they were already at their midday dinner.

Mrs. Dickens looked tired. In the daylight, lines that had not been visible the night before were quite apparent. Letitia was gobbling her food while Fanny watched in disgust. John Dickens was pushing his food about his plate with a fork. Now and then he would raise some to his mouth.

"This *would* be the day that Mary Weller takes her day

off," Mrs. Dickens complained. "She should have known that I would be worn out, but much she cares. Much anyone cares. When I was a girl at home—"

John Dickens's eyes brightened at the sight of young Charles. He pulled out a chair at his side.

"Ah, there is my son and heir. Did you sleep well, Charles, after the—ah—fine reception given your offering last night?"

Charles beamed. Father could make one feel as important as a prince.

"Oh, yes," he said gravely.

Mother gave an audible sniff. Fanny ate stolidly while Letitia continued to gobble. Mr. Dickens gave a tremendous sigh. Then his face glowed with a sudden thought.

"Would you like to go for a walk?" he asked Charles.

The boy almost shouted for joy. A Sunday walk with Father was Charles's favorite recreation. It was better than a magic-lantern show, better than a visit to the theater, better than a meeting of Giles's Cats, as he and his schoolmates called themselves, better even than a giggling conversation with Fan.

He settled down at the table and ate quickly. Then he raised his eyes questioningly to John Dickens.

"Never mind the pudding," Father told him. "We will get an early start in order to enjoy the full benefits of the fresh air and the sunshine, and we—ah—will stop somewhere for tea as we return home."

A short time later, father and son were walking rapidly down Ordnance Terrace away from the gloomy atmosphere of the Dickens dining room. It had been a sharp contrast to the happy air of the night before.

"Shall it be Gad's Hill?" Father asked, setting his tall hat at a slightly rakish angle. The boy nodded. Tilting his own small topper to look as much like Father's as possible, he did his best to keep up with John Dickens's long stride.

"There are times," said his father, "when it is best to leave the ladies to their own devices. This is one of them. On such a day I am grateful to heaven for—ah—giving me a son after my own heart."

Charles was so overcome that he could not answer. He, too, was humbly appreciative to Providence for giving him a father whom he enjoyed, admired and loved.

It was the kind of day one finds only in England in April. The two walked past the Chatham parade ground where red-coated regiments drilled on weekdays. Then they took the road to Rochester and the Cathedral where Charles saw the impressive edifice towering above the town. Beyond the Cathedral they walked on to the short rise known as Gad's Hill. The boy's heart began to pound. Soon they would see The House.

It had been The House to him ever since the first time he had seen it. Not even Father realized the place The House occupied in Charles's heart.

As they walked up the hill, John Dickens was talking in a pontifical manner.

"Of course you know, dear boy, that near this spot the immortal Falstaff robbed the travelers in Shakespeare's *King Henry IV*. The Sir John Falstaff Inn stands on the exact location, I believe—and here we are."

He hastened his steps at the sight of the weather-beaten old hostelry. He thought with pleasure of the "rosy" waiting for him at the bar with a milder drink for young Charles.

He was about to enter the low door of the Falstaff Inn when he realized that Charles was lagging behind. He turned back to the boy.

Charles was standing on the gravel walk, staring at the old red-brick house across the road. Ancient cedars stood along the driveway, and ivy climbed the walls of the house,

F G Kitton

The Sir John Falstaff Inn, Gad's Hill, sketched from Dickens' garden gate

which looked as though it had let down roots and was growing there.

John Dickens touched his son on the arm, but the boy did not notice. He seemed to be in a trance.

"Do dreams ever really come true, Father?" he asked finally. "I have dreamed of owning that house ever since the day I first saw it. Do you think it could ever be *my* house?"

The tall man looked across the way at Gad's Hill Place, then glanced down at his son's rapt face. He put his arm about the boy's slender shoulders.

"To be sure, dreams come true," he replied. "If you work very hard and save your money, someday that house will be yours."

The eight-year-old boy gave a sigh of relief. If Father said he would own The House one day, then he would. It was as simple as that. He turned and followed him into the inn. Meanwhile, John Dickens was rubbing three thin coins against one another in his pocket. He thought they would pay the bill. He hoped so, for he had no others.

The weekend was followed by a succession of dull days. Charles rose each morning, ate his breakfast and set off for Mr. Giles's school. When he returned home late in the afternoon he was too busy with his lessons to notice that his mother kept a pouting, tearful silence.

One evening when winter was coming on, the boy had flung himself on the long horsehair sofa in front of the open fire. The family had finished their meal, and Mary Weller was clearing away the dishes. Mother was upstairs putting Letitia and Frederick to bed, Fanny had gone to a party at a friend's house, and Father was nowhere to be seen. The house was very quiet.

Charles liked it that way sometimes. He was deep in the *Iliad,* which Mr. Giles had lent him that afternoon. The

Gad's Hill Place from the garden

flames crackled and leaped on the hearth, and Charles was aware of nothing but the siege of Troy and the heroes who had stepped out of the pages of his book.

The room grew warmer and he dropped off to sleep. When he awoke, he heard his parents talking, unmindful of his presence on the high-backed sofa.

His mother's voice rose to a whine. "When I married you nearly fifteen years ago, I hardly expected to find dunning tradesmen on my doorstep."

"Now, my dear—" his father's tone was strangely flat— "this is only a temporary state of affairs."

"How long is *temporary?*" his wife shouted. "It has been like this ever since we married. If you didn't insist on entertaining so much—"

"If you knew anything about managing money—" her husband interrupted.

She started to weep. Between sobs, she said: "Do you enjoy moving in Chatham society because your father was a footman and your mother a scullery maid?"

She had touched a nerve. He said sharply: "*My* parents were respectable people who rose in the world from a humble station. My mother, until her retirement, was the trusted housekeeper at Crewe House. And at least neither my mother nor my father, God rest his soul, had to hide on the Continent to escape charges of embezzlement."

Rigid on the sofa, Charles listened. Although the boy had given little thought to the matter, he had supposed that they were prosperous and well connected. Instead, he had just learned, on one side his grandparents had been servants, and at least one of his other grandparents—whom he had thought a civil service employee—was a fugitive from justice. And creditors were trailing his father. So the comfortable, well-to-do atmosphere of 2 Ordnance Terrace was only sham!

A moment later, the front door slammed after John Dickens as he departed, and his wife flounced off toward the rear of the house. Charles, a white-faced little wraith, stole off to bed but not to sleep. The harsh exchange of words he had heard continued to haunt him.

Shortly after that the Dickens family moved. The Brook, a small house on shabby St. Mary's Place, was several steps down the ladder, both socially and economically. Aunt Fanny had married an army surgeon, Dr. Matthew Lamert, who was quartered at Chatham, so of course she did not go with them. But James Lamert, the doctor's son by a former marriage, moved in and became a permanent lodger at The Brook.

Charles was so fascinated by the newcomer that he hardly noticed the departure of his friend Mary Weller, their maid, who had married a dockyard worker. She was replaced by a little drudge from a neighboring institution whom the Dickenses referred to as the Orfling, because that was what she called herself.

If for a time Charles was not aware of the family's descent in the social scale, one reason might have been that at The Brook he had a little back bedroom with sloping walls that held a source of pure delight. This source was books. Somewhere they had been acquired by John Dickens. For Charles they were new friends. As a man he was to write:

From that blessed little room, *Roderick Random, Peregrine Pickle, Humphrey Clinker, Tom Jones,* the *Vicar of Wakefield, Don Quixote, Gil Blas,* and *Robinson Crusoe* came out, a glorious host, to keep me company. . . .

When I think of it, the picture always arises in my mind of a summer evening, the boys at play in the churchyard, and I sitting on my bed, reading as if for life.

To him every spot in the neighborhood stood for some locality made famous in these books. He later wrote:

I have seen Tom Pipes go climbing up the church steeple; I have watched Strap, with the knapsack on his back, stopping to rest himself upon the wicket-gate; and I *know* that Commodore Trunnion held that club with Mr. Pickle in the parlour of our little village alehouse.

Meanwhile the creditors knocked in increasing numbers at the front door of the Dickens house. With several children for whom to provide the necessities of life, John Dickens's financial condition grew no better. But even the uncertain state in which they all lived could not wholly cloud young Charles's world. He still went to Mr. Giles's school and belonged to Giles's Cats, who felt far superior to the fellows who attended other local schools—Baker's Bulldogs, Newroad Scrubbers and the Troy Town Rats.

In spite of the difference in their ages, Charles and James Lamert shared a love for the theater. The young man took the boy to the little Chatham theater whenever he could. In addition, the wide-eyed youngster stood by whenever James and his friends produced amateur plays in empty rooms of the military hospital in Chatham.

And, best of all, Charles and his father still went on their Sunday walks. If the elder Dickens looked a little shabbier now, Charles never noticed, for the man had lost none of his charm for his son.

The next step downward in the family fortunes could hardly have come as a complete surprise, yet it must have been somewhat of a shock to the sensitive boy. Orders came from the main office in London transferring John Dickens to that city. Almost overnight, he sold their household goods and prepared to leave.

On a bright autumn day in 1822, ten-year-old Charles stood in the Chatham inn yard and watched his departing family as they thrust their heads out of the windows of the public stagecoach, "The Blue-Eyed Maid." They were all there—Mother, Father, Fan, Letitia, Fred and the new baby, Alfred. Even the Orfling was going along. Now that they were being delivered from demanding tradesmen, his parents' high spirits were restored. Only Charles, left in the care of Mr. Giles in order to finish out the term, felt disconsolate.

He waved as they called out their gay good-byes. The driver cracked his whip and the stage rolled away. Charles, watching them out of sight, might have felt forlorn indeed except for the strong, comforting arm of Mr. Giles about his shoulders. The boy would remain with him until the end of the term at Christmas, when he would join the others in London.

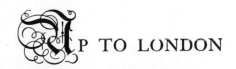

U P TO LONDON

Charles was chilled to the bone and miserable from his cramped traveling quarters when he alighted from the coach in Cheapside upon his arrival from Chatham. A constant downpour had accompanied the passengers during the entire journey. Years later, Charles Dickens wrote that he never forgot "the smell of the damp straw in which I was packed—like game—and forwarded carriage-paid, to the Cross Keys, Wood Street, Cheapside. There was no other inside passenger, and I consumed my sandwiches in solitude and dreariness, and it rained hard all the way, and I thought that life was sloppier than I had expected to find it."

The meeting with Father was a joyful one. They walked all the way to Camden Town, where the family had found a house, for there was no public conveyance and a private cab was out of the question.

Charles was so warmed by the reunion with his father that he scarcely minded the penetrating damp and the gusty winds. Nor did he notice, at first, that they had left the business district and entered streets where the houses became smaller and shabbier.

At last, in Bayham Street, the man stopped before a house that seemed to be the smallest and shabbiest of all. Charles's heart sank as he saw the dingy dwelling in the drizzling December rain.

John Dickens gave a grandiose wave of his hand. "This, my boy," he announced, "is our—ah—domicile. While it may lack the departed glory of—ah—No. 2 Ordnance Terrace or even The Brook, it is, nevertheless, home."

Then Father stooped to enter the low front door. The boy's natural optimism faded as he saw the drab, cramped interior where his sister Letitia and his little brother Frederick were seeing who could make the most noise.

"Be quiet!" Mrs. Dickens exclaimed shrilly. She appealed to no one in particular, "Will someone please quiet those children!"

She seemed to expect no answer to her plea, nor did she receive any. The hubbub and confusion only increased. Mr. Dickens stood helplessly in the center of the room, saying, "Well, my dear—"

Letitia and Frederick threw themselves at Charles with cries of welcome. The newest member of the family, baby Alfred, looked on big-eyed from his mother's arms. After a time, some semblance of order was restored and the Dickenses sat down to their evening meal. Fanny, prettier than ever, had joined them. Since the piano had gone the way of the other household furnishings when they left Chatham, a kindly piano-maker down the street allowed her to practice in his shop.

Mr. Dickens unfolded his frayed napkin with a flourish. "It is good to have our eldest son restored to the bosom of the family."

By now he was waving a large knife over a small joint of meat. "We have missed you sadly, Charles."

Mrs. Dickens dabbed at her eyes with a handkerchief. "You may as well know that your father is having pecuniary difficulties."

"Only for the time being, my love," her husband assured her anxiously. "Something will turn up soon, I am sure."

"In the meantime," she cried, "who will pay the butcher? And the wine merchant? And the greengrocer? And the—"

Charles was glad to escape to the haven of the mean little room on the second floor under the eaves. Father had said it was all his and presented it to him as though it were a suite for a prince. In a sense it was, at least in Charles's mind. Opposite a narrow iron bed there was an oak chest of drawers, topped by a cheap mirror with wavy lines that made his youthful face a blur. Beyond the chest was a rude shelf, and on the shelf were the dear books that had been his in Chatham.

At least *they* had escaped the secondhand dealer. They brought back hopes and dreams he had cherished before coming to London. These hopes and dreams took form now in the question: "Where shall I be sent to school?"

It was a question to which he would receive no answer, although he asked it of his parents more than once. They cut him off each time with errands, odd jobs or silence.

Gradually the idea registered in his mind that they had made no plans for his further education. With that knowledge, the thought of the future opened up before him like a vast chasm.

Charles was not a scholar. He would never be. The world of humanity rather than the world of research attracted him. But when he arrived in London, he was certain that more schooling would enlarge the vista opened for him by his former schoolmaster, William Giles of Oxford. The man had seen in the frail undersized lad, who could never quite keep up with his schoolmates in sports, rare capabilities that would be nurtured by the written word. Fortunately for Charles, in his bedroom under the eaves, those capabilities were now kept alive by his treasured books.

Now the boy entered upon a period of loneliness and neglect that would leave lifelong scars. He was not helped when his sister Fanny received a scholarship at the Royal Academy of Music and was gone from home except on weekends. Charles of course rejoiced at her good fortune. Nevertheless, his heart ached for himself—a youthful slavey who tended the baby, ran errands and blacked the family's boots. He did not even have the company of James Lamert, who had lived with the family for a time after they arrived in Bayham Street. That young man had left them for quarters more suitable to his new position, for he had advanced in the world.

Charles's parents were too occupied with their own pressing troubles to pay any attention to him. As the days passed, they sent him again and again to a neighboring pawnbroker with the household possessions. A few pennies here, a few pennies there, and the soup kettle was boiling again. The first articles to go were the boy's precious books.

One day John Dickens came home from work with a mysteriously happy look on his face.

*Bayham Street in Camden Town, the Dickens home in 1824 as
financial desperation worsened*

"Good news!" he announced triumphantly. "I have seen James Lamert."

Soon after his arrival in London, James had become manager of a blacking factory, where polish for boots and shoes was manufactured. The firm's warehouse was a rambling old building at Hungerford Stairs down on the Thames. It was dirty, decayed and rat-infested. Charles knew it well.

"Your cousin James," said John Dickens, looking at his son, "will give you a position at six shillings a week. You will begin by pasting labels on bottles—not, however, in the front window. Having your interests at heart, he will even assign you lessons and hear them himself at noon."

Charles was too stunned to speak. He had thought of himself as a young gentleman, even though the family's fortunes were at a low ebb. He remembered how the Vicar of Wakefield, one of his favorite characters in fiction, had always said: "Let us be invincible and Fortune will at last turn in our favour."

But how could he, Charles, remain invincible if he fell so low in station as to work side by side with boys from the worst slums in London? He had seen them coming from the blacking factory after work, and a rough crew they were. He could not imagine himself one of them—and yet he soon would be. The thought utterly shamed him.

On the morning of February 9, 1824, Charles, barely turned twelve, reported for duty at the warehouse. From the start he hated everything about the job. The sights, the smells, the company into which he was thrown, and the dirty river framing the whole sordid picture served to make him more downcast. After the first few days James Lamert forgot the lessons and seldom saw him. The boy lost all hope.

Nor did conditions at home improve. His father continued to be pressed on every side for debts. His mother conceived the idea of moving the family into a better house at 4 Gower Street, where she had a brass plate fastened to the front door bearing the words: MRS. DICKENS' ESTABLISHMENT. Young ladies were supposed to seek out the school she had set up, but who the young ladies were or where they were to come from remained a mystery. Nevertheless, for a few days she floated about in a cloud of expectations. In many ways she was as impractical as her husband.

Late in February, 1824, John Dickens was arrested for debt and carried off to the Marshalsea Prison. Fresh shame was added to Charles's burden imposed by the blacking factory.

The distracted Mrs. Dickens solved her problems by pawning their last possession, turning over the key to the landlord and moving into the Marshalsea Prison with her husband, who was still receiving wages from the Navy Pay Office. The Orfling went along to take care of the children. Except for their squalid conditions, the family was better off than they had been for a long time.

With Fanny at the Royal Academy, Charles now became a lodger with an old lady at Camden Town, who took in unfortunate children for a pittance. Now he was alone indeed.

The loneliness was the worst part. At twelve years of age he was completely on his own in the vast city of London without a soul to guide him. Child that he was, sometimes he was unable to resist the stale pastry put out each morning at half price. If he spent his dinner money for it, he went to bed hungry. Finally he hit upon the plan of placing his money in little parcels, each labeled with a day of the week.

At tea time each day, if he had enough money, he went to a coffee shop for bread and butter and a half pint of coffee. If he had no money, he took a walk in Covent Garden Market and stared at the pineapples.

The Marshalsea, scene of John Dickens' imprisonment for debt in 1824

At one time, looking far younger than his twelve years, he went into a public house on Parliament Street and said to the landlord behind the bar:

"What is your very best—the VERY *best*—ale, a glass?" For, the occasion was a festive one, for some reason: I forget why. . . . "Twopence," says he. "Then," says I, "just draw me a glass of that, if you please, with a good head to it." The landlord looked at me in return, over the bar, from head to foot, with a strange smile on his face; and instead of drawing the beer, looked round the screen and said something to his wife, who came out from behind it, with her work in her hand, and joined him in surveying me. . . . They asked me a good many questions, as what my name was, how old I was, where I lived, how I was employed, &c &c. To all of which, that I might commit nobody, I invented appropriate answers. They served me with the ale, though I suspect it was not the strongest on the premises; and the landlord's wife, opening the little half-door and bending down, gave me a kiss that was half-admiring and half-compassionate, but all womanly and good, I am sure.

Sometimes at noon he would play on the coal barges on the river with his companions, Bob Fagin, Mick Walker and Poll Green. The last two resented him, and only with kindhearted young Fagin did Charles experience any sort of friendship.

It was Fagin who felt concern for him when he was seized with the spasms of pain to which he would be subject all his life. There is little doubt that they were physical protests at the unhappiness that flooded his soul, both as a boy and as a man.

When he had a seizure at the warehouse, Bob Fagin made him a rough bed of straw in a dark corner where Charles rolled about in agony. The sympathetic Bob filled empty blacking bottles with hot water and applied them to

Charles's side. Toward evening, when he felt much better, Bob did not like the idea of his returning home alone. This presented problems, as Charles was expected at the Marshalsea that night.

He was too proud to admit that his father was a prisoner there. In front of a house near Southwark Bridge, he shook hands with his companion, thanked him for seeing him home, and ran up the steps. Out of the corner of his eye he watched Bob, who walked slowly and looked back to be sure that all was well.

In desperation, in order to linger until the older boy had disappeared around the corner, Charles knocked at the door and asked the woman who answered if Mr. Robert Fagin lived there. When she shook her head, he thanked her and darted away toward the Marshalsea.

Sundays stood out like oases in his life. On those days he met Fanny, and together they went to the prison. Once the miserable boy broke down and wept at the thought of the lonely week before him. His father was touched, and arrangements were made for Charles to move into an attic in a nearby house and share two meals daily with the family in the Marshalsea.

In April, 1824, John Dickens's mother died. As she had given her younger son financial assistance more than once, his inheritance amounted to less than his brother's, but the 450 pounds he received was enough to bring him out of prison and give him a fresh start.

In May the Dickens family returned to Camden Town to begin life anew. For Charles it was a welcome release from the solitary attic near the prison.

Even in manhood he would bear the wounds of the blacking-factory period, although he kept them hidden from everyone, including his wife and children. But at that early age there was born in him a fierce determination in which he never wavered. That was to pay his debts almost before they were made.

In the words of Mr. Micawber—for whom John Dickens was in many ways a prototype—in *David Copperfield:* "Annual income, twenty pounds, annual expenditure nineteen six, result happiness. Annual income twenty pounds, annual expenditure twenty pounds aught and six, result misery."

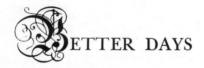 ETTER DAYS

Upon their return to Camden Town, the Dickens family lived in an even poorer, shabbier house than before, but the shadow of the Marshalsea no longer hung over them.

John Dickens went back to work at the Navy Pay Office although he had petitioned to be retired on account of ill health. Mrs. Dickens resumed her role of unhappy, complaining housewife. And young Charles with a lighter heart waited for the word from his father that would remove him from the blacking factory and send him back to school.

He waited in vain. As the weeks went by, the boy realized with an ache in his heart that his parents had no idea of changing his occupation.

By now the warehouse had been changed to a better location in Chandos Street. Here at a large front window, where the sunlight streamed in, Charles was placed with Bob Fagin to tie labels on blacking pots. The sensitive lad's face burned with shame as small knots of bystanders gathered on the street to watch the two boys at their work. Their presence did not seem to annoy Bob at all; in fact, he seemed to enjoy being in the limelight.

One day John Dickens happened to saunter by and saw Charles at his menial work. Perhaps he had not been aware that his son was on public exhibition. At any rate, his fatherly feelings aroused, he was moved to action.

The next morning the boy carried a letter from his father to James Lamert. Charles never knew exactly what was in the letter, although he understood that it carried a protest about his working in the public view.

When Lamert read it, his face turned red with anger. Charles waited anxiously, but he need not have feared. The anger was not directed against him. His employer's voice was kind when he spoke to him.

"This means the parting of ways for us, my boy," he said with regret. "I cannot keep you any longer. Your father—" his tone grew hard—"has insulted me, though the act ill becomes him. I refuse to go on doing him a favor by hiring you."

Charles cried all the way home. His tears flowed partly because he could not bear for anyone to think ill of his father. They were also tears of relief at being delivered of the intolerable burden of the past five months. Never again would he be forced to be a drudge in the blacking factory. Never again would he have to mingle with loutish boys from the slums. Never again would he experience heartbreak at the prospect of a hopeless future. He was free!

John Dickens was coming out the front door as his son went up the walk. Charles told him that he no longer had a job. The man received the news calmly, then set his topper at a triumphant angle.

"I regret that I gave James Lamert an opportunity to discharge you," he declared. "I should have told him that I was removing you from his employ. Come, Charles. We shall go for a walk. And as we—ah—go upon our perambulations, we will reflect upon your future."

As the front door closed, Charles heard his mother's wail. "What will we do without James's help? How can we get along without the six shillings? What is to become of us?"

John Dickens shook his head. "She is the eternal pessimist. Pay no heed to her, Charles. Something is bound to turn up."

Charles's newly found sense of freedom was dashed the following day, when his mother returned in high spirits from a visit to the blacking factory.

"I have fixed everything," she said to her son and her husband. "You, Charles, are to return to work in the morning. Your cousin James was very kind. He spoke quite highly of you."

Charles felt a twinge of the old pain that always seized him when he was in despair. But his father's next words restored him. John Dickens might be impractical, thriftless, happy-go-lucky, but for once he spoke with manly resolution.

"The matter is settled, Elizabeth. Charles will not go back to the blacking factory." He turned to his twelve-year-old son, whose eyes shone with gratitude. "You will enroll at Wellington House Academy in the morning, my son."

School once more! Charles's spirits took an upward swing. But a thought formed within him that would remain all his life. Too young to understand the grinding pressures of poverty, he looked at his mother now in disbelief. "She was warm for my being sent back," he told himself. "My own mother! She was warm for my being sent back."

Wellington House proved to be not much of a school. The headmaster was an ignorant tyrant who ruled with fear and the cane. But there were masters under him who could teach if a boy wanted to learn.

Not that Charles had an overwhelming thirst for knowledge. His chief interest lay in finding the boyhood he had lost. He did it well. Not a word about the blacking-factory days passed his lips, and no one seeing the handsome boy who carried his curly head so proudly would have recognized the miserable little drudge of Hungerford Stairs. His schoolmates knew only a jolly, ruddy-cheeked youngster of medium height who went into gales of laughter at the slightest cause or no cause at all. He bore little resemblance to that waif who had drifted alone about the streets of London.

Like most of the boys, Charles was neither very good nor very bad at his studies. There is no evidence that he excelled in Latin, mathematics, French or any other subject.

But along with the other boys, he made capital use of his leisure time. He built toy theaters, for which he painted gaudy scenery. Sometimes the actors were white mice trained "better than the masters trained the boys." One white mouse "ran up ladders, drew Roman chariots, shouldered muskets, turned wheels, and even made a very creditable appearance as the Dog of Montargis. He might have achieved great things, but for having the misfortune to mistake his way in a triumphal procession to the Capitol, where he fell into a deep inkstand, and was dyed black and drowned."

Charles and the other young rascals walked about the

streets, talking in their own private speech which they hoped would be mistaken for a foreign tongue. Once they pretended to be beggars and asked alms from some old ladies. When the ladies were opening their pocketbooks, the scamps burst out laughing and took to their heels.

The two and a half years during which Charles was a day pupil at Wellington House passed rapidly. He wrote for the school paper; he made friends, indulged in all the mischievous tricks which a growing boy can think of and succeeded in part in forgetting the misery of his factory days.

Then suddenly it was 1827. School was behind him. Through a relative of his mother, he found employment as an office boy in a lawyer's office. Then he became a clerk in another legal office in Gray's Inn, where for centuries lawyers—or solicitors, as they were called—had followed their profession.

The work was dull and the pay was poor. True, there were bright moments. He could lean out of a second-story window, drop cherrystones on the heads of passersby and draw back before he was seen. When someone came upstairs to complain, he was the soul of innocence. The departing visitor was certain that such a gentlemanly boy could not have been the offender.

This job, however, was only for the moment. Charles was looking ahead. When he had seen his father enter the Marshalsea, the boy vowed that someday he would be rich. Fifteen shillings a week, which were his wages, did not mark the road that he intended to follow.

For two years now, John Dickens had been a parliamentary reporter for the *British Press*. Finally forced to retire from the Navy Pay Office because he had been arrested for debt, he had discovered this new means of livelihood. It was no trivial achievement to be a parliamentary reporter.

When Parliament was in session, a reporter earned almost fifteen guineas a week.

To Charles, this amount seemed princely riches. He decided that he, too, would become a parliamentary reporter. Having a streak of hardheaded practicality, he kept his job in Gray's Inn, but bought a book and commenced to learn shorthand.

The title alone, Gurney's *Brachygraphy,* would have discouraged many a lesser young man, but it only drove Charles onward. For months he struggled.

Yet he would never allow life to be all work and no play. By now Fanny had graduated from the Royal Academy of Music. With friends she enjoyed musical evenings, and Charles joined them. He still loved to sing.

He had another interest, too—the theater. His well-developed gift of mimicry would have led him there even if he had not discovered a fellow clerk whose enthusiasm for the stage was almost as great as his own.

Each had just turned sixteen. Conscious of their new-found status, they began to dine in low-priced restaurants and to smoke cheap cigars after dinner. Going to the theater was the next logical step.

There were many kinds of theaters in London. There were the "major" theaters at Covent Garden, Drury Lane and the Haymarket, which were allowed by law to present only the spoken drama. And there were the "minor" theaters, which could not present the offerings of the major theaters from October to May. They managed to get around the rules by throwing in a few songs and calling their presentations "burlettas." Any of these theaters admitted playgoers to the galleries at half price after nine o'clock. This reduction appealed especially to young gentlemen earning fifteen shillings a week.

Most exciting of all were the theaters across Westminster

Bridge that presented varied entertainment from sensational drama to side-splitting comedy. There was no lack of theaters for young gentlemen who wished to frequent them.

Anywhere and everywhere, there were "private" theaters where would-be actors might "tread the boards" for a fee. It is likely that Charles Dickens—who as a man could never decide whether writing or acting was his greatest love—knew these theaters from actual experience.

Meanwhile, Charles was improving in his lessons in the *Brachygraphy* book. He had now advanced so far that he felt he could give up his position in the solicitors' office in Gray's Inn and take a place instead in Doctors' Commons.

Doctors' Commons was not only a repository for various important legal documents such as wills and deeds; it was also a hodgepodge of courts. When a court was in session, the services of a free-lance shorthand writer were often desired, and Charles was now a free-lance shorthand writer. Although the job was uncertain, he thought it would pay better in the long run than that of clerk, which he had just left. However, it did not pay fast enough to satisfy him. The ambitious youth had a good reason for wanting money as fast as he could get it. He was in love.

IRST LOVE

Charles was seventeen when he first met Maria Beadnell in 1829. His friend, Henry Kolle, was engaged to Anne, Maria's sister. Kolle had talked so much and so often about the charms of his auburn-haired betrothed that he hardly mentioned her two sisters, though Charles was aware that they existed.

He was happy to accompany Kolle one evening to the Beadnell home on Lombard Street. Mr. Beadnell was a banker and an important personage. Charles Dickens was a young man on his way. He was not at all certain which way, but definitely somewhere that led away from poverty, uncertainty and that dreadful period deep in his memory which he was trying desperately to conceal even from himself.

As the door of the house on Lombard Street opened, Charles drank in a scene of wealth and opulence. He had a glimpse of shining rosewood furniture, soft velvet drapes and a fashionable drawing room with Mr. Beadnell and his plumpish wife standing in the center of it. Modishly dressed, gay, laughing guests circled about the room.

Charles straightened his stock, held his proud head higher and, with no warning whatever, walked straight into heaven.

An angel—he found out shortly that her name was Maria Beadnell—was seated in the corner by a tall, graceful gold harp. Her little hands wandered in and out of the shining strings in a manner that went straight to his heart. She was a tiny thing, coming just to his shoulder, as he discovered later. Her brown eyes and her ringlets, arranged in the fashion of the day, enslaved him from the moment he saw her.

In a daze, he acknowledged an introduction to his host and hostess. Mr. Beadnell shook his hand pompously, and Mrs. Beadnell, her nose a trifle in the air—its customary position—muttered something indistinct.

"—to meet you, Mr. Dickin."

Later he would resent her mispronouncing his name and wonder if she did it on purpose, but tonight, as far as he was concerned, everyone was perfect.

Finally he found himself before his goddess. There were several other adoring slaves as well. Among them he recognized William Moule in his usual gorgeous tie, William's

Maria Beadnell, Dickens' first love (the model for David Copperfield's Dora)

brother Joe with curling mustachios and a scarlet waistcoat, and Arthur Beetham, buttoned up to the chin to keep out imaginary drafts. Charles lamented that there would always be young men standing about Maria Beadnell.

The girl attracted young men as honeysuckle draws hummingbirds. The constant presence of young men at the Beadnell house testified to that. Anne was promised to Henry Kolle, and the eldest daughter, Margaret, was engaged to a young tea merchant. Thus there was a clear field for Maria, and she had no idea of narrowing it anytime soon.

On that first night of their meeting, John Dickens's eldest son was radiant with joy. Bowing over the little hand she extended to him, he had lifted it to his lips. For a wild moment he thought of tearing off his new yellow gloves, the better to feel those fingers, but he restrained the impulse and smiled down at her instead.

She asked with a practiced air, "Where have you been, Mr. Dickens? Why haven't I met you sooner?"

She was a year older than he, as he was to learn. His heart pounded as he answered her, and he thanked heaven that his voice kept its normal tone.

"It has been my loss, Miss Maria. Shall we make amends for the situation by seeing each other often?"

She tapped him coyly on the wrist with her filigreed-ivory fan. "Naughty Mr. Dickens!" She gave an appealing look at the other men. "Don't you agree? Isn't he naughty?"

From that night on, Charles moved into another world, though from necessity he continued as a free-lance reporter in Doctors' Commons. He waited with other youths like himself until he was hired to take down a case. In his spare moments—of which there were too many to suit him—he worked at improving his shorthand. Also, he became a visitor on a reader's ticket at the great library of the British Museum. There he read Addison, Shakespeare, Goldsmith and

Dickens at eighteen

others. He knew that they would be valuable additions to his short formal education.

By now he was making more than the fifteen shillings a week that he had earned as a clerk at Gray's Inn. He never neglected his duties in Doctors' Commons—his determination to keep free of financial difficulties was a lodestar that led him on. But after hours he lived. He was a regular visitor to the house on Lombard Street, where, to his dismay, there was a steady stream of other young men. He was seldom alone with his idol, but he was grateful just to sit and look at her. To pass a few words with her now and then threw him into a state of rapture.

His adoration extended even to her little white spaniel Daphne. Maria would shake her curls and fondle Daphne while Charles and the other admirers looked on enviously. Ah, fortunate Daphne!

One day Maria sent him to the shops to match a pair of blue silk gloves. He bore them back to Lombard Street as though he were carrying the Holy Grail.

As the months went by, Charles began to feel at times that his beloved was accepting him and even returning his devotion. Marriage was uppermost in his mind, but he dared not speak. How could he, when his only means of livelihood was his work at Doctors' Commons? All he could do for now was to exchange little notes and small gifts with her. He loved her very much.

Nearly two years had passed since their meeting. Sometimes he felt that Mr. and Mrs. Beadnell—especially Mrs. Beadnell—did not look upon him with favor. One day in March, 1831, he met the three girls shopping with their mother. They were on their way to the dressmaker. Charles needed no bidding to fall into step beside Maria and escort them to their destination. There he held wide the door for them to enter. Holding her nose a trifle higher than usual,

Mrs. Beadnell swept through. Then she gave him a curt dismissal.

"And now, Mr. Dickin, we'll wish *you* good morning."

Startled, Charles retraced his steps and reviewed in his mind the recent behavior of Mr. Beadnell. Had that gentleman become cold and distant?

Charles shook his head. Perhaps he was only imagining things. It was easy to fancy slights when Maria was so enchanting and he was so much in love.

One cold day in late 1831 he called at Lombard Street to find both Mr. and Mrs. Beadnell absent. Maria received him in the morning room where a fire burned cheerily on the hearth. Her eyes were red and her satiny cheeks were blotched. For once she paid no attention to Daphne, who lay neglected in her basket.

Charles tried to take Maria in his arms. "What is wrong, my darling?"

She pushed him away. "No, Charles. You mustn't."

"Why not?"

He tried to gather her closer, but she resisted him. For a moment she seemed almost distant, but he thrust the thought away. His love, his own Maria, was suffering, and he was suffering with her.

"Tell me," he pleaded. "If anyone has hurt you—"

She led him by the hand to a small plum-colored sofa and seated herself beside him. He was distressed beyond measure at the pitiful face she turned up to him.

"Papa is taking us to Paris tomorrow."

"Paris!"

The cry burst from him in anguish. Paris was at the ends of the earth. The English Channel would lie between him and Maria. This could not be happening, he must be dreaming.

"Papa says I need to complete my education," Maria

went on. "I don't think that is the real reason. He believes you and I are seeing too much of each other, and he is determined to put an end to it. We will remain for a year."

The impetuous young man kissed her again and again. "He shall not separate us. I did not mean to speak so suddenly, Maria, but I love you. We shall be married, and then he cannot carry you off to Paris."

Maria held him at arm's length and studied him. He could not define the expression in her eyes, but apparently she could not see a husband in the smooth-faced, pink-cheeked boy before her.

"What would we live on?" she asked at last.

His arms dropped to his sides and he turned away without a word. Even Maria was touched by his misery.

"Oh, Charles," she whispered.

He took her in his arms again and pressed her head against his shoulder. She seemed to be the child and he the parent, although the opposite was much closer to the truth.

"Never mind, my little one," he murmured. "The time will pass somehow. I love you, I adore you. I will work from early until late while you are gone. They can't separate us forever."

The two parted before her parents returned. The grieving Charles had no desire to see them. He wanted to remember the Maria who had welcomed his caresses. It did not cross his mind that she had failed to voice love for him. On her part it had been passive acceptance.

The Beadnells soon sailed for France, and Charles felt that a part of him had been wrenched away. He was certain that Maria was enduring the same sorrow.

Now the iron will that was to become a fixture in his life asserted itself. He must have money for the day when their separation ended. He was still too young to be a parliamentary reporter, but he let it be known through every possible channel that it was the position he desired above all others.

Meanwhile he turned to acting. For three years he had been to the theater nearly every night. It was a passion that would last all his life. At this period he turned to the stage in a desperate effort to make a livelihood for himself and his wife-to-be. If his family and friends thought well of him as an actor, why would a larger audience not feel the same? He even got an engagement with the manager of one of the major theaters, but when the day came he was ill with a terrible cold and an inflamed face.

Another door opened unexpectedly. Two doors, in fact. A new evening newspaper, the *True Sun*, got under way, and from the beginning Charles Dickens was on its staff. He was accepted also as a reporter on the *Mirror of Parliament*, edited since 1828 by his mother's brother, John Henry Barrow. The *Mirror of Parliament* was in early nineteenth-century England what the *Congressional Record* is to the Congress of the United States today.

By the time Maria returned from Paris, Charles had gone far in journalism. In spite of his youth, his natural ability was rapidly making a name for him among older and more experienced reporters. On the *Mirror of Parliament* he was a sort of assistant editor with the responsibility of hiring other staff members.

His devotion to the absent Maria had kept him at two jobs. His spare time he spent in private theatricals. By now he was not only an actor; he could be producer, director, stage manager, designer, musician, dramatist and even a carpenter if the occasion demanded. He was almost twenty-one. Like his old friend, the Vicar of Wakefield, he had persevered. Surely Fortune would at last smile on him.

Fortune seemed kindly enough disposed, but Maria was

not. At her suggestion, they had written seldom. The time, she had said, would pass faster that way.

When Maria came home, Charles found her cold and unapproachable. Whenever he visited Lombard Street, Mr. Beadnell was present. It almost seemed as if he were determined to keep Charles from seeing Maria alone. The young man was sick at heart.

He found ways to send notes to Maria, who seemed willing enough to receive them and even to reply. Undoubtedly the coquettish side of her nature thrived on such interchanges.

When Charles came of age on February 11, 1833, his family gave him a party. They lived now at a better address, and they made a grand occasion of the affair. His sisters and brothers were all present—from Fanny and Letitia down to Augustus, who was only five and greatly excited at being allowed to stay up. There were hired waiters and many guests, Mr. and Mrs. Beadnell among them. And of course there was Maria.

Charles at last made an opportunity to get her alone and express ardent emotions he had been storing up during her absence. He forgot the slights, the misunderstandings, the indifference she had displayed. Tonight he was a man, alone with the girl he loved.

He poured out his feelings, sure that their relationship would be restored to the old basis—or what he had felt to be the old basis.

Maria stared at him as if he were almost a stranger. She slipped out of his arms and glanced at the door.

"Oh, Charles, can't you realize that is all ended? Maybe I once thought I was in love with you, but that was more than a year ago. After all, you are only a boy."

He was stunned. For this he had labored at three occupations and spent sleepless nights! In that moment, Charles Dickens had a bitter awakening.

He held the door open for Maria to pass through. It was late and the guests were leaving. With an effort, he collected himself and went forth to play the role of the eldest son in whose honor the party was given.

At long last he stumbled upstairs to bed. Ten years ago, his childhood had seemed without hope and light, but that had been nothing compared to what he was enduring now.

He sat down on the side of his bed and buried his face in his hands.

"Only a boy!" he exclaimed harshly. "What a short and dreadful word. If this is coming of age, I had rather be back at Hungerford Stairs!"

HE YOUNG REPORTER

About the time that the affair with Maria ended, Charles Dickens had resigned from the *True Sun,* which was in financial difficulties. He kept on with his work for the *Mirror of Parliament,* but was still forced to fall back on free-lance work at Doctors' Commons when Parliament was not in session.

Scarcely a day passed that the young man did not cast wistful eyes toward the great daily newspapers of England,

especially the *Morning Chronicle,* a strongly liberal organ
and the rival of the London *Times.* In spite of the efforts
of his uncle—John Henry Barrow, editor of the *Mirror of
Parliament*—to get him a position, he was not hired. Then,
the next year, the *Morning Chronicle* underwent an extensive reorganization that resulted in new ownership and a
new editor.

Charles Dickens was recommended by a reporter friend,
Tom Beard, only recently engaged himself, as "the fastest
and most accurate man in the Gallery." Day after day and
even night after night, Dickens and Beard had sat together
in the Strangers' Gallery in the House of Commons to take
shorthand notes of the proceedings and later to transcribe
them for the *Mirror of Parliament.* Although Charles was
scornful of the slow manner in which legislative bodies
moved—even when his own party, the Whigs, was in power—
he performed his duties faithfully and well. The result was
that he was offered a job on the *Morning Chronicle.*

It was a period of social change in England and politics
held the center of the stage. Charles, leaning forward eag-
erly in the Gallery of the House of Commons, with his
shorthand pad on his knee, listened to speeches of many
kinds. As time went on, he realized that the evils he hated
—filth, poverty and crime in the workhouses, factories,
mines and slums—were only symptoms of what was wrong in
a social structure that depended on the exploitation of the
workingman and other helpless people. In years to come he
would be offered a seat in Parliament more than once. Each
time he would turn it down because he knew he could
criticize with more effect as a private citizen. Now, as a
young man, he grew more and more to despise the cumber-
some activities that went on in "the great dustheap of
Westminster," as he called Parliament.

It was a time when the public was showing concern for

intolerable working conditions, child labor, prison reform and slavery. Charles Dickens knew where he stood. He was against the Tory diehards and for the rising radicals who favored a change in the management of the country's affairs. In the future he would become a writer on social problems; right now he was choosing sides.

They were exciting days. When Parliament was not in session, Charles and the other reporters were sent out by their papers to cover speeches, elections and other news in the boroughs and counties. In the 1830's there was no telephone or telegraph. The railroad was in its infancy. Traveling was a matter of mail coaches, private post chaises and saddle horses.

Charles vied with the others to be first to get the news to his paper. His life was a succession of attending meetings and taking shorthand notes, narrowly escaping injury whenever a wheel flew off a post chaise, galloping through the night on treacherous roads and, more often than not, arriving first with his story at the office of the *Morning Chronicle*. Frequently he wrote his assignment on his knee by the light of a lantern as the carriage bounced and bumped along a country road.

He held his own with the other newspapermen, some of whom were much older. In his own words, he made a great splash. One of the veterans in the field said: "There never *was* such a shorthand writer."

For a time he still lived at home with his family on Bentinck Street. Young Henry Austin, who was to marry Charles's sister Letitia, and Tom Beard, his reporter friend, were often there. So was Tom Mitton, who had been a clerk with him at Gray's Inn and was now a lawyer. And a young composer named John Hullah, a friend of both Charles and Fanny. She was studying music again at the Academy. And there were amateur theatricals, of course.

Broadstairs in the 1830's

Anyone meeting young Dickens on the street would never have suspected the deep wound inflicted by Maria Beadnell. In 1833 he sported a handsome new cloak with black velvet facings, which he threw back over one shoulder in the Spanish fashion. He was always fond of good clothes, and he liked them showy. It was a trait that would lead his rival Thackeray to say on one occasion; "Dickens was never quite a gentleman."

At twenty-one he walked with a spring that was almost a swagger. It was the mark of a youth who intended to let nothing stop him. The flame of life burned so brightly in Charles Dickens that every morning was a new day, and every hour held new expectations and fresh discoveries.

Still, there was something that darkened these bright days. John Dickens was, as usual, living beyond his means to satisfy his expensive tastes. Although he was employed by the *Morning Herald* and was well paid, he still borrowed.

Late in 1834 Charles found that his father was in the hands of a bill collector. The son emptied his pockets of ready cash, borrowed more from a friend until payday, and went to the old man's rescue. But that was not the end. A few days later, John Dickens was arrested by a firm of wine merchants and placed in a sponging house, where he had twenty-four hours to make arrangements for paying his creditors.

It was Charles who made the arrangements. He managed to give a promissory note and obtain money for the family's immediate difficulties. When the debts were cleared away he talked matters over with his father. It was almost as if he were the head of the family, and John Dickens was the erring son.

"It's all right, Governor," Charles told him. "We will weather the storm. I'm moving you and Mother and the children—the girls, too, of course—to cheaper lodgings. I've taken a top-floor back at Furnival's Inn for Fred and me. We will set up bachelors' quarters. It would be too crowded in your new lodgings for all of us."

Mr. Dickens twisted his hands nervously. "I'm sorry. The bills just kept piling up—"

Charles put his hand on his father's shoulder. "Forget it, Governor. Everyone has a little hard luck now and then. But watch those pounds and shillings, sir."

"I will. Oh, I will," John Dickens promised. He seemed tremendously relieved to find that his son bore him no ill will.

The young man clapped him on the back and went on his way whistling. He was determined to see everything in as bright a light as possible. The truth was, he had expected all this for weeks. He knew his father's salary at the newspaper office and he knew his parents' mode of living. The two did not agree. It was comforting to know the blow had fallen and was over with. Besides, Charles had another reason for optimism.

Back in 1832, he had made up his mind about something. For some time he had been writing sketches about people and places. Some of them he thought were very good.

One evening, a manuscript in his hand, he walked up to a letterbox in Fleet Street, and dropped the manuscript into it. It was addressed to the *Monthly Magazine,* a publication that did not pay for material, but gave would-be writers an opportunity to see their unsigned work in print.

Several weeks later, Charles had gone into the bookshop of Chapman and Hall and asked to see the December, 1832, issue of the *Monthly Magazine.* With shaking hands, he thumbed through the pages. There it was!

Tears sprang to his eyes. Charles Dickens was a Victorian, and Victorians were unashamedly emotional. He dropped a half crown on the counter and walked rapidly out the door before his tears fell.

He could hardly bear the crowded street. He went down Whitehall and turned into Westminster Hall. There in its dark shadows he walked until he was calmer. This was his high moment. This was his hour.

With the knowledge in his heart that he was truly an author, he could go out to meet the world. It was a world of competition and pressure, a world where he was soon to realize that he must be the father of that man-child, John Dickens. It was a world where his young dream of love was to be shipwrecked. But it was also a world where the novelist Charles Dickens would come into his own. He knew it then, in Westminster Hall.

After his initial appearance in print, he continued to write for the *Monthly Magazine*. By August of the next year he was using the signature "Boz," a family nickname. The magazine's readers were beginning to look for the sketches which flowed from his pen under that name. Charles Dickens was beginning to feel the literary power stirring within him. That was why, in 1834, not even the near-disaster of his father's second arrest for a debt would dim the glory of that moment in Westminster.

CHARLES GOES COURTING

The name "Boz," which was creating a stir in English literary circles, had an interesting history. For years little Augustus, the youngest child in the Dickens family, had been dubbed Moses for the overly trustful son in *The Vicar of Wakefield*. The bearer of the name pronounced it "Boses." The word was soon shortened in family circles to "Bose" and, finally, "Boz." When the time was ripe, Charles Dickens adopted it for his own name.

Early in 1835, the owners of the successful *Morning Chronicle* decided to launch the *Evening Chronicle*. Its editor, George Hogarth, who had been an associate of Charles on the morning paper, lost no time in asking the young reporter to write some sketches for the new one. He felt the name of Boz would sell many copies of the paper.

Charles was quick to agree. At the same time he asked modestly whether they did not think he "had any claim to *some* additional remuneration (of course, no great amount) for doing so."

They did think so. His pay was increased from five to seven guineas a week. He continued to dash furiously about the countryside as a reporter, generally scooping his opponents. Then he would return to his lodgings at Furnival's Inn to create the brainchildren teeming in his mind.

Month by month the sketches increased in number and at last grew into a project that caused Charles, mentally at least, to caper for joy. It came through his new friend, Harrison Ainsworth, the well-known young English novelist.

Ainsworth's home at Kensal Lodge was a gathering place for English men of letters, and Charles felt tremendously honored to mingle with them and with artists such as Daniel Maclise and George Cruikshank.

There he met Ainsworth's publisher, John Macrone, who said that he would like to publish Boz's sketches in book form. Like one of his later creations, Barkis in *David Copperfield,* Charles was willing.

Accordingly, the arrangements were made. Charles would write enough additional sketches to make two volumes. Macrone would publish it early in 1836 and give him 150 pounds for the copyright of the first edition. As a crowning glory, the famous artist Cruikshank agreed to illustrate *Sketches by Boz,* which is what they decided to call it.

By this time another era had begun in his life. Charles was an engaging young man, and George Hogarth took him home to meet his family. The small house in Chelsea was filled with Hogarths—father, mother and seven children. Their guest found them all delightful.

George Hogarth at fifty felt the kinship of similar tastes with his young associate. During the next seven months he published twenty of Dickens's offerings in the *Evening Chronicle*. They were word pictures of London life as the young man had seen it, and they ranged from street scenes, gin palaces and pawnshops to Astley's Circus and Greenwich Fair. He was no longer writing for the *Monthly Magazine,* because that publication did not pay.

Meanwhile, Charles was becoming more and more welcome in the Hogarth home. He was giving Robert shorthand lessons, being charmed by little Georgina, and realizing that clear-eyed young Mary Hogarth understood him best of all.

And Catherine? Some say she caught him on the rebound after the affair with Maria had ended. At any rate, the nineteen-year-old girl with the rose-petal complexion, heavy-lidded blue eyes and an inclination to plumpness soon had the young man captivated. Or was he in love with love? Who knows?

Unlike the Beadnells, who had always looked upon him with a slight disdain, the elder Hogarths made him heartily welcome. The girls admired him; the boys, who were younger, appreciated him. Charles basked in such an atmosphere. There was always music and laughter and peace in the Chelsea house. It was a welcome change from his parents' crowded rooms and his own sometimes lonely bachelor quarters.

In 1835, he found himself engaged to Catherine—or Kate, as he always called her. He loved what he regarded as

Georgina Hogarth in her later years

her appealing innocence. There were others who regarded it as an exasperating slowness, but Charles was in no position to see that.

The courtship went smoothly except when Kate felt that he was neglecting her. She believed it all too often, if one may judge from the spells of sullen pouting by which she punished him. He tried to reason with her and tell her that a writer's time was not his own, especially for a young writer who had his way to make. She was hard to convince. The letters that passed between them would indicate that she did not understand and he was none too patient.

February 7, 1836, was his twenty-fourth birthday. It was also the day that saw the publication of *Sketches by Boz,* illustrated by Cruikshank. It was a happy time in both the Hogarth and the Dickens families. The book received favorable reviews and the author was especially gratified by "Hogarth's beautiful notice" in the *Morning Chronicle.*

A happier time was just around the corner. On February 10, a caller rapped on the door of Charles's third-floor flat in Furnival's Inn. The young man opened the door and stared out at a small birdlike man in the hall. Before the man could present a card, Charles gave a shout.

"You're the man who sold me the issue of the *Monthly Magazine,* which carried my first story!"

The visitor stepped back, startled by Charles's enthusiastic welcome.

"I am William Hall, the junior partner of Chapman and Hall," he said.

"Come in, come in!" Charles urged. "Also you were acting as a clerk the day I bought the magazine in your shop on the Strand. I'd know you anywhere!"

Hall entered and gave up his hat and walking stick. He peered nearsightedly at Charles.

"Why, bless me! You *are* the young fellow who thumbed through my magazine and then looked as if you had won first place in a lottery."

Charles laughed. "I had won a better prize than that."

Hall continued to nod like a mechanical toy. "Well, well, well. This must be a good omen, my dear sir. I came here to discuss a little matter of business with you, but I assure you that I had no idea the young man in my shop was Boz."

Charles moved an easy chair nearer the fire for Mr. Hall. He sat down himself, all attention. Business meant writing, writing meant money. And money—enough of it—meant marriage to Catherine Hogarth.

"You may be aware," Hall began, "that the artist Robert Seymour is preparing a series of sportsmen's plates about some characters known as the 'Nimrod Club.'"

Charles nodded. In journalistic circles he had heard mention of such an undertaking, but he had given the matter little thought. To him the written word was of first importance. The art of the stage was a close second. Other things were secondary.

"It has occurred to my partner and me," Hall went on, "that you may be willing to furnish the text that will accompany the plates. We will pay you a handsome sum. Say, fourteen guineas a week."

Charles's blue eyes grew larger. He was making only seven guineas a week on the *Chronicle*. The two salaries would make him a good living and speed the day of his marriage to Kate. Indeed, with twenty-one guineas, there would be no reason to postpone it.

"I'll take it," he said in a tone that he immediately feared was overanxious.

"Good." His visitor arose and picked up his hat. "I shall inform Mr. Chapman. You may expect your first assignment tomorrow."

"Just a minute." Charles planted himself in the path of the departing publisher. The thought crossed William Hall's mind that he had never seen a person so completely alive.

Charles Dickens wore his hair in the mode of the day, slightly long and brushed down over the forehead on one side. His blue eyes, his rosy cheeks, his mobile features gave him a striking appearance.

"A handsome youth," the publisher thought. "Perhaps his hair is a *little* longer, his eyes are a *little* bluer, and his features a *little* more expressive. That is the difference."

Charles's words came out in a rush. He was speaking now in a deadly serious tone, not at all like a carefree young man about town. His cronies at the theater—his fellow reporters in the Gallery—the well-known men such as Ainsworth, Cruikshank, Macrone and Maclise, who were beginning to be his friends—none of them would have recognized him.

Here was a cool, keen, quick-witted man of business, eager to please, but unwilling to compromise. He was very sure of himself. He had come a long way from the fearful youth who had dropped his manuscript in a postbox in Fleet Street on a dark night late in 1832.

"Mr. Hall, I must insist on a certain amount of freedom in my work," he said. "I must confess I am not too well acquainted with sports, but surely that does not matter. Every annual and sporting magazine in England is filled with texts and illustrations of clowns and comics disguised as sportsmen. They have become almost commonplace."

Mr. Hall waited. He almost admired the young man's impudence.

Charles went on. "I know England, sir. As a reporter, I am familiar with every city, town and hamlet in the land. I know the countryside. I know the roads. I know the inns. I know the people of every sort and condition. Give me a free hand to take the Nimrod Club where I will. Mr. Seymour will find an abundance of scenes to illustrate, I assure you."

Why, the young man was actually saying that Seymour should follow him, not he Seymour. Hall smiled at the audacity—and waited.

"Now, there's the question of publication," Charles continued. "I would suggest that the book be brought out in monthly issues for a shilling apiece. Many people will part with a shilling twenty times who cannot pay a guinea and a half for a book. They will have a bargain, too, for the total price will be less than that of a standard volume. Then, if it goes well, you can always publish it in book form at the end. There is little risk, Mr. Hall, and the prospect of a great deal of profit."

Mr. Hall was listening with interest and respect. Here was a hardheaded man of business, not an addlepated writer.

The publisher was only partly right. Charles Dickens was many men and would continue so throughout the years. He was indeed a man of business, his early environment had taught him the importance of that. He was a writer, though far from being an addlepated one. He was an actor. He was a lover. Even now, with every character he created, he took that character's form and shape in his mind. He was many people. He was humanity.

Hall was nodding agreement to the young man's proposition. "Interesting," he murmured. "Most interesting. You understand, of course, that I must consult my partner. You will hear from us soon, Mr. Dickens. That I promise you."

The upshot was an agreement, on Charles's terms, between him and the firm of Chapman and Hall. Within two days the author had sat down at his desk, and *Pickwick Papers* was born.

With the increased income, nothing stood between the

young couple and marriage. Preparations for the wedding went on with dispatch. Charles and Kate would live at Furnival's Inn in the apartment he had leased earlier for three years.

Except for the fact that Kate still indulged in spells of pouting when her intended husband's duties kept him away from her, Charles lived in a rosy glow of life and love. If Maria had slashed at his innermost being, the scars were buried deep. It was springtime in 1836, and the wedding would take place on April 2.

T FURNIVAL'S INN

On April 2, 1836, Charles Dickens and Catherine Hogarth were married at St. Luke's Church in Chelsea, with only the immediate families and two other guests present. They were Tom Beard, the best man, and John Macrone, who had published *Sketches by Boz*. Henry Burnett was present, too, but he was as good as married to Fanny and therefore almost family.

After a simple wedding breakfast at the Hogarth home,

with healths drunk all around, the newly married couple set out in a rented carriage for Chalk, a tiny village not far from Chatham where Charles had lived as a child. There, in a tiny cottage, they would spend their honeymoon.

They had only a week, which was all the time Charles could spend away from his work. It was a happy time. They drove about the country and Charles showed Kate the scenes he loved—the Cathedral at Rochester, the parade grounds at Chatham, the Dover Road, an old red-brick house set back in a grove of cedars.

"That is Gad's Hill Place," he told her. "My father used to bring me here on walks when I was a little boy. We are now on Gad's Hill, where Falstaff met the robbers in *King Henry IV.*"

Perhaps both of them were glad to return to London and Furnival's Inn. The two were city-bred. Charles thrived in an atmosphere of publishing offices, noisy streets and many people. Kate was happier in familiar surroundings where the members of her family could frequently come and go. As time went on her husband was to discover that he had married not only a wife, but the entire Hogarth clan.

The Dickens quarters in Furnival's Inn must have been a little crowded for Charles and Kate, young Fred Dickens and Mary Hogarth, who soon came to live with them. Charles did not find the rooms cramped at all. In later years he would look back at that period when he worked in "a sympathy more precious than the applause of the whole world" as the happiest time of his life.

One evening, soon after Charles and Kate returned from Chalk, the publisher William Hall brought Robert Seymour to Furnival's Inn. Charles was hard at work on the second number of *Pickwick Papers* (the first had been published on March 31), and he had asked the artist to submit a second design for "The Stroller's Tale," as he had not liked the first.

The meeting did not begin well. Seymour was unhappy and showed it. He had been unhappy ever since Pickwick had supplanted the Nimrod Club.

"But I am a *comic* artist, Mr. Dickens," he insisted. "I simply cannot draw the sketch for the Dying Clown. Now if we went back to my idea—"

Charles and Hall looked across him at each other. They had settled weeks ago on the plan of *Pickwick Papers*. The publishing firm was fully agreed to it. Seymour must accept it, but how to make him do so was another matter.

Charles rose, poured drinks around, and passed them in the manner of a seasoned host. "My own mixture," he told them with pride. He drank deeply from his own glass and sat staring at it for a moment. Then he looked up.

"Mr. Seymour, I was quite pleased with your drawings for the first number," he said. "You did yourself proud. I refer to the sketches of our friend, Mr. Pickwick, in particular."

The older man appeared somewhat appeased, but still looked unhappy. Charles went on.

"But the picture of the Dying Clown is quite another matter. It is all wrong. The woman should be younger. The 'dismal man' not quite so dismal. And I implore you not to make the sick man so repulsive. Do you follow me?"

Apparently Mr. Seymour had no notion of following him. He only shook his head and insisted once more that he was a comic artist.

In the end he yielded—people generally yielded to Charles Dickens—and left with the promise that he would try again.

The footsteps of the two men had hardly died away on the stairs before Kate burst in from a bedroom and Fred from the kitchen.

"What a disagreeable man!" Kate exclaimed, and Fred agreed.

Charles was sitting on the sofa, mopping his forehead with a half-comical air. "Whew!" he exclaimed. "That was an ordeal."

But the real ordeal was yet to follow. Seymour went home, tried once more—unsuccessfully—and then walked into his summerhouse and blew his brains out.

The news hit Charles hard. He was a sensitive person, and felt a deep sense of blame for the act of the unfortunate man. None of Boz's associates blamed him, however. Seymour's act was clearly the result of an unbalanced mind, as his farewell note to his wife showed.

There were other reasons, too, for Charles's anxiety. The future of *Pickwick Papers* hung in the balance. Would Chapman and Hall go on with the serial? What would happen to young Mr. and Mrs. Charles Dickens, who had married on the strength of the assignment? There were some troubled moments for the residents of Furnival's Inn, third-floor back.

Those moments did not last for long. Chapman and Hall did not miss a single publication. The second number of *Pickwick Papers* came out with the three engravings that Seymour had completed, and the publishers let it be known that they were looking for another artist.

Cruikshank was too busy. A young man by the name of William Makepeace Thackeray did not quite fill the bill. Neither did Robert William Buss, who already had a reputation as an artist.

At last a man was found. He was Hablôt Knight Browne, who won Charles's heart with his etching of Mr. Pickwick and Sam Weller in the yard of the White Hart.

Boz held the sketch at arm's length and studied it carefully. At last he turned to the artist, who was several years his junior.

"It's perfect!" he declared. "You are a genius, Browne. I tell you, it's just as though my mind had guided your hand. It's Mr. Pickwick to the life. And Sam Weller! You have caught the impudent, jolly Cockney look. I'll wager the public will take Sam Weller to their hearts."

The younger man blushed with pleasure. It was rewarding to hear his efforts praised, especially by the successful Boz.

Then Charles frowned. He held the drawing closer while the other watched nervously. What had he found?

"I see you signed it 'Nemo,' " Charles said. "Somehow I don't like that. If I am Boz, your pen name should match mine. Boz and—and—" He snapped his fingers in triumph. "I have it! Boz and Phiz!"

Hablôt Browne beamed. The man's enthusiasm was contagious. Suddenly Browne found his hand seized and pumped violently up and down.

"Shake on it to seal the bargain. What a team we shall make! We go together like sugar and cream—bacon and eggs—" Charles paused for words and then burst into infectious laughter. "—Dickens and Browne!"

And so the undertaking that had begun as a moderate success mushroomed into a triumph even on the other side of the Atlantic. Victorian readers were captivated by the adventures of Mr. Pickwick, Mr. Snodgrass, Mr. Winkle, Mr. Tupman and the faithful Sam Weller. Three months after Charles's marriage, in a letter to Macrone, he added a postscript: PICKWICK TRIUMPHANT.

The ambitious young man was going full speed ahead. He was never so happy as when he had several irons in the fire; and as he usually had numerous irons in the fire, he was happy most of the time. He was still with the *Morning Chronicle,* although he would soon resign. He and his friend John Hullah, the composer, were doing an operetta, *The*

Village Coquettes, which would be produced at St. James's Theatre, with the famous tenor Braham in the cast. Charles was dramatizing his story "The Great Winglebury Duel" as a play called "The Strange Gentleman." Now he promised Macrone a three-volume novel, although *Pickwick Papers* was far from finished. And a second series of *Sketches by Boz* was due in October.

As though all that were not enough, Charles became involved—quite willingly, it must be admitted—in another venture. The publisher Richard Bentley was starting a new magazine, to be called *Bentley's Miscellany.* He offered Charles the post of editor and the young man accepted. He promised also to write a novel to run as a serial in the *Miscellany.*

On January 6, 1837, Kate gave birth to a boy at Furnival's Inn. The parents named him Charles, and in due time he became Charley. But in those first wonderful days the young father addressed him and spoke of him as The Phenomenon.

By now Charles was a busy editor. The first issue of the *Miscellany* had come out just before the birth of Charley. It was an instant success. Its contributors included many of the editor's friends, his father-in-law, George Hogarth, and some of the best-known writers of England.

In the pages of this new publication, Dickens signed his name as "The Inimitable Boz" at the end of letters to numerous correspondents.

In February, his new novel, *Oliver Twist,* began to run serially in the *Miscellany.* This offering was very different in tone from *Pickwick Papers.* The latter had been all jollity and hilarious adventure. *Oliver Twist* began in a workhouse and progressed to the lowest slums of London.

More and more Charles Dickens was developing a spirit of social consciousness—an "I *am* my brother's keeper" attitude. His own boyhood in the blacking factory under the shadow of the Marshalsea Prison furnished its beginning. When innocent young Oliver wandered the filthy haunts and alleys of London and later fell in with the rascally Fagin and the criminal Bill Sikes, the author knew whereof he wrote. He had experienced such a background at the age of twelve and he had visited it later as a reporter.

His anger against injustices to the poor was beginning to burn white-hot. From early manhood Charles Dickens was a humanitarian. In *Oliver Twist,* first serialized in 1837, he began to voice his creed.

By this time he was a family man, with many friends, prominent men, who could scarcely be expected to climb the stairs to the third floor of Furnival's Inn. His annual income had reached eight hundred pounds. Clearly it was time to look for more fitting quarters. He could afford them now.

 MOVE UPWARD

They found a house at 48 Doughty Street, just north of Gray's Inn. It was a warmly pleasant-looking dwelling of pink brick, with three stories and an attic. It was in fine condition from top to bottom, from its white-arched front door to its trim garden in the rear.

Doughty Street was a quiet, middle-class neighborhood with a gate at one end and a lodge with a porter at the other. To the four people (five, if one counted Charley) who moved into the pink-brick house, the twelve rooms were indeed spacious after the crowded third-floor flat at Furnival's Inn.

Because Charles loved people, the door was never closed. His writer friends came frequently, among them John Forster, whom he had met at Harrison Ainsworth's on Christmas Day. Charles's younger sister Letitia dropped in often with Henry Austin, her husband-to-be, and Fanny with Henry Burnett. The house echoed with voices and laughter.

Close on the heels of the move to Doughty Street came the first anniversary of the publication of *Pickwick Papers.* As a tribute to its success, Chapman and Hall made him a gift of five hundred pounds over and above the amounts they had promised to pay him. Then they gave a great dinner in his honor.

To them Charles wrote: "If I were to live a hundred years and write three novels in each, I should never be so proud of any of them as I am of Pickwick, feeling as I do that it has made its own way, and hoping, as I must own I do hope, that long after my hand is withered as the pens it held, Pickwick will be found on many a dusty shelf with many a better work."

Scarcely more than a year ago he had been a struggling writer. His rise had been swift. In the language of the man on the street, he was sitting on top of the world. This state of affairs was not to last for long.

The Dickenses were fairly well settled in the new house by early May, 1837. One Saturday night, Charles, Kate and Mary went to the St. James's Theatre. As they returned home and entered the house, Charles looked proudly at his two "petticoats," as he called them. Kate, beautiful as a full-blown rose, and Mary, graceful as a young willow, were a decided contrast. Both were necessary to give him the sense of completeness that filled him tonight. Kate was his

The Fleet Prison (where Mr. Pickwick was incarcerated)

wife, his adored one, the mother of his child. Mary was peace, rest, contentment, understanding. Mary was—just Mary.

He sank down on the long sofa and patted the cushions invitingly.

"Do sit down," he urged the two women. "Talking an evening over is the best part of it."

Kate was walking toward their bedroom at the rear of the house. "Wait until I get into something loose. I've been trussed up like a chicken long enough."

Charles laughed. His young wife's plumpness was a part of her, and he loved her for it. Slim little Mary was dear to him in a very different way. She was a child, in spite of her sixteen—no, seventeen—years, who rounded the circle and made his and Kate's world complete. And yet she was not a child, Charles reflected a little sorrowfully, as he watched her standing at the foot of the stairs, gentle, lovely and un-awakened. One of these days some fellow would discover her and carry her off. Charles hoped the fellow would be worthy of her, but he doubted it.

No, she was certainly far from being a child. Charles felt that she had a wisdom beyond her years. She understood him when he did not understand himself. She sympathized with him when he was in a bad mood. She was happy when his spirits were high. She pointed the way onward when his human frailties were all too apparent. His feelings toward her did not conflict in any way with his love for his beautiful Kate.

He watched Mary now as she started slowly up the winding stairs. Slight of body and small of bone, she seemed almost dreamlike as she moved upward.

"You're not leaving me, too," he exclaimed in mock dismay.

"Kate will soon be back," she assured him. "I am very tired, Charles. I can't stay up another minute."

Mary Hogarth

He followed her with his eyes as she went on up the stairs. Dear Mary! He wondered if she knew how much they all depended on her. She saw that domestic affairs ran smoothly; she kept the servants on an even keel; she was the heart of the household. He adored his beautiful, slow-thinking Kate, but he knew that she was in reality a child and Mary a woman. Yet it all seemed right, and he was content.

A brief, strangling cry from above hit him like a bolt of lightning. He stiffened for a moment and then raced for the stairs. Kate, clad in a dressing gown, had just appeared in the doorway.

"Did I hear someone call?" she asked.

He threw her a frightened look. "It was Mary!"

Together they reached her bedroom, where they found her on the floor. They knew she had been stricken with some terrible illness, but she could not speak. Charles turned anguished eyes to Kate. "Find Fred! Tell him to run for a doctor!"

He raised the girl in his arms and held her. It seemed hours before the doctor arrived. He examined her and shook his head. Murmuring something about a tired heart, he turned away.

Her battle for life was brief. She grew steadily worse through the night and died at three o'clock the following afternoon. Charles had never left her side.

He was alone with her at the end. Kate and her father were downstairs attending Mrs. Hogarth, who was coming out of one fainting spell only to go into another.

As Charles looked at the still form on the bed, he sobbed. So young, so fair, so full of life only last night! He could not believe that she was gone. In his grief he slipped a ring from her hand and slid it on his little finger.

"It shall remain there as long as I live," he whispered to himself.

They buried her in Kensal Green Cemetery; Charles had prepared the inscription for the tombstone:

MARY SCOTT HOGARTH

DIED 7TH MAY 1837

YOUNG, BEAUTIFUL AND GOOD

GOD IN HIS MERCY

NUMBERED HER WITH HIS ANGELS

AT THE EARLY AGE OF

SEVENTEEN

Kate and he were badly shaken by Mary's death. They went away to a secluded spot in the country, where they remained for two months. There was no new installment of *Pickwick Papers* or of *Oliver Twist* during that time. The days and weeks passed, and the sorrowful couple comforted each other until they felt they could return to Doughty Street once more.

But life must go on. By now John Forster had become Boz's unofficial business manager. That summer he introduced Charles to the great actor Macready, who would soon become one of the Dickens circle.

In November the publishers Chapman and Hall gave a banquet for the increasingly popular young writer at the Prince of Wales Tavern in Leicester Square, "to celebrate the completion of England's most popular work of fiction."

In the course of the evening, the headwaiter entered and placed on the table a gigantic cake bearing a little figure of Mr. Pickwick. Mr. Chapman and Mr. Hall then presented the guest of honor with a check for 750 pounds. The little boy in the blacking factory had come a long way.

As the year drew to an end, the christening day of little Charley Dickens rolled around. Miss Angela Burdett-Coutts was his godmother. She was an heiress whom Charles had met several years earlier. Because the two shared a burning desire to help the poor and underprivileged, they established a lifelong friendship. She was to prove herself a generous friend to the entire Dickens family.

When the baby was presented at the christening font, his parents intended that he be called Charles Culliford. However, when the clergyman asked for the baby's names, his excited grandfather, John Dickens, exclaimed "Boz!" As a result, the infant's name was entered on the church register as Charles Culliford Boz Dickens.

Early in 1838 Charles made preparations to begin a new book. The idea had been in the back of his head for some time. As far back as his Chatham days, he had heard about the miserable conditions of the Yorkshire boarding schools. On January 30 he and Hablôt Browne—Boz and Phiz—were passengers in the mail coach that left the Saracen's Head in London. They would see conditions in Yorkshire for themselves.

After a two-day journey they arrived in the moorland country in a blinding snowstorm. In spite of bleak, desolate surroundings, they found themselves comfortably quartered at the George and New Inn near Bowes Academy, the school for which they were looking.

In the morning, Charles faced Browne at breakfast across a lavish table. It was spread with toast, cakes, Yorkshire pie, a generous slice of beef ("the size and much the shape of my portmanteau," Charles groaned), tea, coffee, ham and eggs.

"If this is typical of Yorkshire, I fear the reports we have heard are greatly exaggerated," Browne observed.

"They will not be exaggerated," Charles answered gloomily. "I have heard too much."

By midmorning they had arrived at Bowes Academy, a large, square, austere building on the edge of town. Ushered into the headmaster's office, the friends waited with their tale well prepared. At least Charles was well prepared. Browne intended only to sit by and watch his actor friend.

Presently a tall, rawboned giant of a man, with a black patch over one eye, advanced into the room and looked at his visitors suspiciously.

> *Fee-fi-fo-fum—*
> *I smell the blood of an English-mun!*

thought Charles.

"Good morning, gentlemen. What can I do for you?" the one-eyed giant inquired.

"Mr. Shaw, I presume?" Charles asked courteously.

"The same," the giant acknowledged.

"I am Henry Bradshaw, sir, of London," Charles informed him. "Mr. Johnson here and I have come on a matter of business. I am representing a widow—her husband was distantly related to me—with a twelve-year-old son whom she wishes to place in a good boarding school. Your school was recommended to me."

"By whom?" Mr. Shaw inquired with interest.

Browne squirmed, but Charles went on smoothly.

"Someone in my club," he answered. "A group of us were talking one night when your name was mentioned. An acquaintance—I forget his name—said that Bowes Academy turned out a good brand of scholar."

The headmaster's good eye made an almost imperceptible motion. Was it a wink, or did Charles fancy it?

"The boys toe the mark or we turn them out," their host informed them. "I suppose you wish to tour the school?"

"If you would be so kind," Charles said.

For forty-five minutes the headmaster led them through the halls and grounds of the academy. It was a grim, forbidding place, but not even Charles's sharp eyes could ferret out any evidence of mistreatment or cruelty.

They thrust their heads in at the doors of several class-rooms. The boys studying at battered, carved-up desks seemed neither ill nor abused. One bright-eyed little fellow closely watched Mr. Shaw, the visitors and the master. When he thought no one was observing him, he played with a wooden puzzle. Charles felt a pang. The boy made him remember his own days at Wellington House.

Back in the office, once again William Shaw confronted his visitors. Charles imagined there was a triumphant gleam in his eye.

"I trust you have seen enough to satisfy you," he told them. "The classrooms, the sleeping quarters, the kitchen, the dining room. And I assure you that outdoor sports have their place in good weather."

A short time later, the travelers from London were riding away from the school in their hired rig. Charles shook his head.

"I don't like that man," he said. "I don't know how he managed to present the school under a good light, but there is not a word of truth in all he says."

"Oh, come now," Browne said amiably. "You have no proof."

"No, but I will," Charles returned doggedly. "In my opinion, Mr. Shaw is a rascal of the first order."

Next, they delivered a letter of introduction from a lawyer friend in London to a Yorkshire attorney. They found Richard Barnes a jovial, ruddy-cheeked old fellow who seemed to know little or nothing of the Yorkshire schools. From him they also preserved their identity and presented themselves still as men from London aiding a widow in finding a school for her son. The old man appeared honest but somewhat ignorant. He gave them letters of introduction to two local schoolmasters.

That night at the inn, before retiring, Charles and his friend reviewed their day. So far their journey had been fruitless. Browne pulled off a boot and tossed it in the corner.

"You'll just have to go home and make up your villains out of whole cloth," he declared.

Charles scowled. "I won't do it. My characters are real people. Oh, I disguise names and places and events, but all my people and my plots are true. You do recognize the difference between truth and fact, Browne?"

The question remained unanswered. There came a heavy knock at the bedroom door. The two men looked at each other. They were expecting no visitor.

"Come in," Charles called.

The door flew open, and in tramped the lawyer whose acquaintance they had made earlier in the day. There was a frown on his jovial face and he seemed perturbed.

Charles rose to his feet. "Why, Mr. Barnes, what brings you here?"

"A simple regard for human beings," the old man blurted out. "I couldn't go to bed with summat on my mind."

In his agitation he had lapsed into the native Yorkshire speech. He continued now, looking back uneasily over his shoulder. "I wouldn't want my neighbors to think ill of me, but I must speak up. I know the Yorkshire schools from top to bottom. They are not fit for decent animals, let alone humans. If you have any influence with his mother, don't let the little lad you spoke of come here. He will be bullied, beaten, starved and whipped. The churchyard is full of the work of the scoundrels. He had better remain ignorant all his days than learn what he will learn in the Yorkshire boarding schools."

Charles Dickens looked at his traveling companion. "I told you so," he said harshly to Browne. "I told you so."

Within a week Charles was home again. With a reporter's

skill, he had unearthed enough evidence to give him material for half a dozen books. But only one was necessary. *Nicholas Nickleby* would arouse all England and awaken the public to the evils of the boarding-school system of that time.

Less than a month after Charles returned from Yorkshire, Kate gave birth to her second child, a girl. It is not surprising that they named her Mary.

When summer came, Charles took a cottage at Twickenham for his wife and babies. Visitors streamed in and out, among them his father and mother, his younger brothers, Fanny, Letitia, Henry Burnett and Henry Austin. There were Charles's friends, too—Bentley, Hullah and John Forster, who was becoming the author's *alter ego*—his other self.

That year he finished *Oliver Twist*. It was his first book to be published under his own name rather than his pen name of Boz.

For him the greatest honor of the year was his election to the Athenaeum Club. Only men of some accomplishment belonged to it. Charles Dickens was only twenty-six when he was made a member. Forty other men were admitted at the same time, one of them being the great naturalist Charles Darwin.

Dickens's twenty-seventh birthday had barely passed when he realized that he must come once more to his father's rescue. No other course remained. Unknown to his son, John Dickens had borrowed small amounts of money and piled up a considerable debt with Chapman and Hall. He had even sold sheets of his son's old manuscripts as souvenirs, but that had failed to help. He had extended himself in every direction and was about to be arrested again.

When Charles heard the news, he took command at once. He decided to settle his parents and young Augustus in Exeter, away from the temptations of the city.

Dickens in 1839, from the "Nickleby Portrait" painted by
Daniel Maclise

He found a little white cottage, which he filled with good secondhand furniture. Then he sent for his father and mother, confident that this was a good place for the "Governor." Within a month his two old "children" were unhappy and complaining; but Charles was firm. As long as John Dickens lived, his son would be paying his debts. Charles took it all in stride. He had a deep affection for his father, and as the years passed he even forgave his mother for once being "warm" to sending him back to the shoe-blacking factory.

The year ended in a flurry of events. In September he completed *Nicholas Nickleby*. On October 29 a third child —Kate Macready, named for her mother and Charles's actor friend—arrived in the Dickens family. Once again they were bursting out of their living quarters. As the year ended, Charles was again going through the throes of house-hunting.

1 DEVONSHIRE TERRACE

In December, 1839, the Dickens family moved to 1 Devonshire Terrace. It was, in Charles's words, "a frightfully firstclass Family Mansion, involving awful responsibilities."

At the age of twenty-seven Charles Dickens was already a famous writer and, like other well-known men of his day, a frequent visitor to such fashionable addresses as Gore House, fashionable gathering place for the London men of letters, and Holland House, a noted Whig stronghold.

But it was old Samuel Rogers's little gem of a place at 22 St. James that came most often to his mind as he considered improvements for Devonshire Place. Samuel Rogers, poet, banker, man of means and patron of the arts, was a bachelor who knew what he wanted. Whenever Charles attended his small exclusive breakfasts, he admired the art treasures and literary mementos that his host displayed against a background of elegance.

Long before the move from the Doughty Street house, Charles was in a flurry of ordering new suites for the drawing rooms and bedrooms of the Devonshire Terrace residence. He must have remembered with considerable pain how he and Mary had sallied forth, while Kate was indisposed before Charley's birth, to buy furnishings in the secondhand shops for the Doughty Street house. Now he alone was involved in choosing draperies and upholstery, luxurious carpets that sank down when one walked on them, and gleaming mirrors that reflected the rich furnishings. He had the plain doors of the house replaced with paneled mahogany, and the wooden mantels with carved Italian marble.

The library was also Charles's study, and he gloried in the row after row of volumes bound in finely tooled leather. Yet none of them, he knew, could rival the charm of the cheaply bound books of his childhood when he first made the acquaintance of Tom Jones, the Vicar of Wakefield, Robinson Crusoe and Don Quixote.

The imposing three-story house, with its stately entrance, its graceful stairs and its rich drawing rooms, was a fitting background for a man who had earned it. The mansion was a symbol of success, as were the carriage and the horses in the stables. Charles Dickens sat at his desk directly in front of the window overlooking the garden in the rear. There he could see his children at play. At times he would put down his pen and go joyfully out to join them.

When he sat down at his desk he shut out the everyday world and entered a world of his own. It was a world for which all his readers have been the richer ever since.

The Old Curiosity Shop and all its characters—Little Nell and her grandfather, Dick Swiveler, the Marchioness (no other than the Orfling come to life again) and the odious Quilp—were born on that desk. So was *David Copperfield,* the book he called "my favorite child." In many ways it is his own story. Maria Beadnell, of course, is Dora. John Dickens, always waiting for something to turn up, is Mr. Micawber, and Charles's mother is Mrs. Micawber. Barnaby Rudge and his raven Grip in the novel *Barnaby Rudge* had their beginning there, too, while the real raven, for whom Grip is named, strutted and cawed outside in the garden.

In 1840 Charles assumed the editorship of a new periodical called *Master Humphrey's Clock.* He had broken with Richard Bentley by this time and completely cut himself off from the *Miscellany.* The new magazine proved successful, but skirted near-disaster at the start. Charles had in mind a collection of stories that would be loosely tied together by the figure of an old man who kept manuscripts deep in the compartment of a grandfather's clock. As the story progressed, the old man would take the manuscripts out to read.

The public would have none of it. They clamored for another full-length novel by their literary idol, Charles Dickens. He had intended the "child-story" of Little Nell for one issue of the magazine. Now, to please his readers, he extended it to book length.

With the passing of the weeks, in his mind Little Nell became Mary Hogarth. As he wrote he traveled every step of the way with his central character, for through her Mary lived again. To a friend he wrote: "Dear Mary died yesterday when I think of this sad story." When he realized that

Dickens in 1840

in the course of the story Nell, too, must die, he could hardly bring himself to write the death scene. It brought back too vividly that tragic time in Doughty Street.

The Old Curiosity Shop swept the land like a torrent. Its fame spread to America, for he was as well known there as at home. It is said that several thousand Americans waited on a dock at Boston for the sailing ship bringing the current copies of the magazine. As the captain brought his ship into port, they called out with one voice: "Is Little Nell dead?"

Even *The Old Curiosity Shop* finally came to an end, but by that time each number of the periodical was selling 100,000 copies. The issue of *Master Humphrey's Clock* for January 9, 1841, announced that Dickens's next book would be *Barnaby Rudge*.

This story had been in his mind long before he began *Oliver Twist*. His slowness in delivering it had been one of the outward causes of his break with his publisher, Richard Bentley. Charles was relieved beyond measure when Chapman and Hall, the publishers of *Pickwick Papers,* bought the rights to *Barnaby Rudge*.

The background of this new novel was the Gordon Riots of 1780, incited by Lord George Gordon. In a sense, the book is a forerunner of *A Tale of Two Cities* with its background of the French Revolution. Although Dickens is seen as deploring mob violence and the overthrow of authority, he obviously rejoices with the rioters when they burn Newgate Prison. (There speaks the horror of prisons, a feeling acquired in his childhood.) Throughout *Barnaby Rudge,* the reader feels the author's sympathy with the oppressed.

The plot of *Barnaby Rudge* is weak. The story gets off to a slow start, and critics place it at the bottom of the list. Yet one of its heroines, Dolly Varden, stepped straight out of the pages of the book into the hearts of Englishmen. Even today the mention of a "Dolly Varden" dress brings to mind a girl in a large beribboned straw hat and a flowered frock with pointed bodice and panniered skirt.

As *Barnaby Rudge* progressed, the fourth Dickens baby was born in the Devonshire Terrace house. He was called Walter Savage Landor, for the leonine old poet who had first listened to the idea that grew into *The Old Curiosity Shop.* (Charles Dickens named all his sons for writers.)

In April Charles and Kate were off to Edinburgh, where a royal welcome awaited him. *Barnaby Rudge* was well on its way, and with its completion, *Master Humphrey's Clock* would cease. Meeting a weekly deadline was proving too strenuous.

The trip to Edinburgh was a great success. The novelist and his wife, having been wined and dined and duly admired, came back to London in July. Kate had never wished to go in the first place. She and Charles were both true Londoners; the city was where they wished to be. The difference between them was that he frequently became restless and wanted to go to parties, plays, dinners, entertainments of any sort. She would have been content to live quietly at home for the rest of her days. The situation did not make for happiness, for Charles Dickens was electric, outgoing, ambitious and dynamic.

From childhood he had sided with the suffering and the downtrodden. The writing of *Barnaby Rudge* had only strengthened this attitude. About this time he became deeply concerned over the truly terrible situation of child labor and the horrible living conditions of the poor. As he studied the mines and factories of England, his anger against the privileged classes became white hot.

A trip to America was the next logical step. Although he himself was a member of the middle class and rejoiced in

Catherine Dickens, Dickens' wife, from the portrait by Daniel Maclise (1842)

his position and possessions, he hated snobbery and the privilege of the ruling few. It seemed to him that England was enslaved by corruption and privilege. To him, in 1841, America seemed a shining example of liberty and democracy. Perhaps someday his own country would go in that direction. Meanwhile he must see the New World.

There he would go—with Kate, of course. Furthermore, it was gratifying to be granted a holiday of fourteen months with 150 pounds a month, to be deducted from future earnings. Why, he could write a book about America! Perhaps he might even start the three-volume novel he had promised Chapman and Hill for 1843. The bright path of the future stretched invitingly before him.

N AMERICA

In October, 1841, Charles wrote his friend John Forster: "I have made up my mind (with God's leave) to go to America."

With the ever present restlessness urging him on, he booked passage on the *Britannia* for himself and Kate and her maid Anne. At first he thought he would take the children—all four—but when he thought of six people in one small cabin for two weeks, he decided against the idea.

Kate did little protesting. Perhaps she had learned long ago that there was little use in protesting to Boz, who swept family, friends and acquaintances before him whenever he was determined upon a course of action. He was so alive, and she was so yielding—and so dull.

Kate cried quietly until it was time to embark. The artist Daniel Maclise, who is said to have been in love with Kate when she was a girl, had painted a group watercolor of the children for the parents to take on their journey. During the couple's six months away from England, Fred Dickens, the young uncle whom the youngsters adored, would have charge of them at first. Then the actor, William Charles Macready, who was a close friend of Dickens, would take the children into his home, where he and his wife would care for them.

Charles and his wife sailed from Liverpool on January 4, 1842, on a voyage that proved to be the line's stormiest in years. Even Charles was distressed by seasickness, and Kate was the picture of misery.

One night when the boat was grinding and creaking so that the passengers were positive that each new plunge into the raging sea would be the last, Charles looked across the cabin at Kate, who lay weakly in the opposite bunk. His usually rosy face was pea-green, but there was a ghost of laughter in his voice.

"If this keeps up, Kate, our children can collect the insurance I took out before we left England and be the richer for a thousand pounds."

"Oh, Charles, how can you laugh at a time like this?" she wailed.

Poor Kate was slow to appreciate humor even when it seemed appropriate, so she could have been excused when the whole Atlantic Ocean seemed to be pounding at the portholes.

The Dickens children in 1841, painted by Daniel Maclise

Charles closed his eyes. "Sometimes it is better to laugh than to cry," he told her in a pained voice.

After fourteen days at sea the *Britannia* docked for seven hours at Halifax. The brief period was long enough for the officials to give Charles a public welcome. It was only a forerunner of things to come.

When the ship arrived in Boston, not only were the reporters there to meet Boz; the newspaper editors were there as well. A modern world, sated by celebrities, can hardly imagine the honors showered on Charles Dickens.

Staid old Boston, the cultural center of the United States in 1842, turned out for him. There were receptions, there were dinners; there were balls, breakfasts, invitations to private homes. Boz was the lion of the hour, and he loved being lionized. He struck up a warm friendship with the poet Longfellow, who was five years his senior, and urged him to visit England. A year later the American accepted the invitation.

The high point of the Boston visit was a great dinner at Papanti's with tickets at fifteen dollars. ("Three pounds sterling!" in Dickens's words.) Some people thought this occasion was marred by Boz's reference to the need for an international copyright agreement, a subject close to his heart. While literary works were being pirated in both countries, the extreme popularity of Dickens's works perhaps made him feel the injustice a little more than some other writers did. He spoke in moderate terms, but some of those present felt that his complaint was ill-timed—that a guest should not refer to his financial loss at a social gathering in his honor.

After Boston, Charles and his wife went on to Hartford, Connecticut, where at a public dinner he spoke in even stronger terms about international copyright. This time the press attacked him, and Boz's anger was aroused. Despite advice from friends, he declared that he would *not* keep still, he would *not* beat around the bush, he *would* speak up for justice.

In spite of the unfavorable newspaper publicity, New York welcomed him warmly. The Boz Ball at the Park Theatre was an occasion long to be remembered. Streamers of bunting hung from a golden rosette overhead. Each box was trimmed in white and gold. Between the tiers of boxes were, among other decorations, medallions representing Dickens's works. A large golden Maypole arose in front of the orchestra and blazing illumination was furnished by two great chandeliers and lesser lights. The effect was rich, and Charles basked in the atmosphere.

On the stage there were *tableaux*—living pictures—showing scenes from Boz's books. The *pièce de résistance* was the appearance on the stage of Charles and Kate, escorted by the Mayor and his wife. The crowd that night, not including gate-crashers, numbered three thousand.

At the Dickens Dinner a few days later, over which Washington Irving presided, Boz referred again to international copyright. This time he had a different audience. They approved of the "bright-eyed young man with lots of long, curly, brown hair, and big, laughing blue eyes," and that approval grew no less when Charles made his speech.

With just a reference to the copyright question, he went on to praise Washington Irving, whose writings he had long admired. The next speaker, Cornelius Matthews, defended Dickens's copyright stand and said it was nothing more than right.

Although most of the New York papers ignored the speech, Horace Greeley's *Tribune* came to its defense. The cause for which Charles Dickens had argued had at least been recognized, and a problem recognized is halfway to being solved.

The *Tribune* editorial read:

We have heard murmurs that Mr. Dickens has ventured to allude, in his replies to complimentary addresses, to the gross injustice and spoilation to which he and all Foreign Authors are exposed in this country from the absence of an International Copyright or some other law protecting the rights of literary property. We trust he will not be deterred from speaking the frank, round truth by any mistaken courtesy, diffidence or misapprehension of public sentiment. We ought to speak out on this matter, for who shall protest against robbery if those who are robbed may not? Here is a man who writes for a living and writes nobly; and we of this country speedily devour his writings, are entertained and instructed by them, yet refuse so to protect his rights as an author that he can realize a single dollar from all their vast American sale and popularity. Is this right? Do we look well offering him toasts, compliments and other syllabub, while we refuse him naked justice?

It does very well in a dinner speech to say that fame and popularity and all that are more than sordid gold—but he has a wife and four children, whom his death may very possibly leave destitute. . . . But suppose him rich, if you please, the justice of the case is unaltered. He is the just owner of his own productions as much as though he had made axes or horseshoes, and the People who refuse to protect his right ought not to insult him with the mockery of thriftless praise.

Philadelphia was the next stop. Then Washington, where he had an audience with President Tyler and the former Vice President, John Quincy Adams, who wrote a charming little poem for Kate. From there Charles and his wife proceeded to Richmond and Baltimore, then westward on a course that took them through Pennsylvania, down the Ohio River, and up the Mississippi as far as St. Louis.

Charles's first impressions of America were not his last. Although he had been enthusiastic during the early days of his visit, he was cooling off. In a letter from New York to his friend Macready he wrote: "This is not the republic I came to see; this is not the republic of my imagination."

Perhaps this change of feeling was partly due to his visits to certain American institutions. In Boston he had been pleased with his tour of the Perkins Institute for the Blind under the guidance of its director, Dr. Samuel Gridley Howe. And he was delighted with what he saw on a trip to the factories and mills of Lowell.

But New York was another matter. The Lunatic Asylum, the Alms House, the Island Jail were bleak, dirty and odorous—like "a thousand old mildewed umbrellas wet through, and a thousand dirty clothes-bags, musty, moist, and fusty."

Escorted by police officers, he visited the slums one night and found them fully as loathsome as the slums of London. He thought that the prison known as The Tombs was even worse. He came away in disgust, feeling that America could teach England nothing in the way of prison reform.

To add to his dissatisfaction, he felt he was overcharged by hotels. Moreover, he found too many crude and ill-bred people who regarded him as public property and would give him little peace night or day. He was beginning to discard the rosy view of America with which he had begun the trip.

One Americanism he despised was the chewing and spitting of tobacco. His *American Notes* are filled with mention of the repulsive habit. Nor was that all he deplored on his voyage by river steamer down the Ohio. He found the craft dirty and crowded, as well as filled with bores and pests who gave him no privacy. Later the hero of his novel *Martin Chuzzlewit* would travel down the Ohio and be subjected to the same discomforts.

But all was not loss. Boz thought Cincinnati a beautiful place that had arisen out of the forest like an Arabian Nights city, although even there, at a party in his honor, he met "at least one hundred and fifty first-rate bores." By

Steamer "Messenger" on which Dickens traveled down the Ohio from Pittsburgh to Cincinnati

this time he was frankly homesick for the more compact country from which he had come. Certainly he longed for English faces, English speech and English people, together with the camaraderie of long walks, horseback rides and intimate little dinners with old friends whom he missed immeasurably.

After Cincinnati the next stop was the Galt House in Louisville. "A splendid hotel," said Dickens, "where we were as handsomely lodged as though we had been in Paris, rather than hundreds of miles beyond the Alleghenies."

Soon the travelers reached St. Louis, which was as far west as they would go. From there they retraced their journey by water as far as Cincinnati. In that city they hired a private carriage in which to make the journey east over the prairies. From Sandusky, Ohio, they boarded a boat to Buffalo and Niagara Falls. Their American journey was drawing to a close.

And none too soon. Both Charles and Kate were intensely homesick for their children. Charles had discovered that he was more British than he had realized. There was much that was good about America—friends such as Longfellow, Irving and others; the oysters as big as plates, but Charles knew that he was English to the core. The wonderful American Utopia of which he had dreamed did not exist.

In his last letter home to his friend and adviser, John Forster, Charles wrote:

"As the time draws nearer we get FEVERED with anxiety for home . . . kiss our darlings for us. We shall soon meet, please God, and be happier and merrier than ever we were in all our lives. . . . Oh, home—home—home—home—home—home—HOME!!!!!!!!!!"

OME AGAIN

It was late at night when the hackney coach rolled up to Devonshire Terrace. Charles helped Kate to the ground and flung a sovereign for the driver to Fred, who appeared at the front door with every evidence of having dressed hastily. Then Charles and Kate rushed to the nursery.

The four children were fast asleep. Mamey in quiet repose reminded her father of that other Mary. She had grown more like her during the six months that had passed.

Katey lay with her arms flung above her head. Not without reason was she nicknamed "Lucifer Box"—she was quiet only when she was asleep. In disposition she was more like Charles than any of his other children. The baby Walter had flung off the bedclothes and was a bundle of soft disarray.

Kate began to sob loudly. The noise awakened their eldest son, Charley, who leaped out of bed, crying "Mama!" Mamey rose to her knees and peered sleepily through the bars of her crib. Then Katey awoke and the baby, roused from his slumbers, held out his chubby arms.

Charles and Kate laughed and cried together. The four children swarmed over their mother and father on the sofa and vied with each other in planting kisses on their parents' cheeks. Soon curly-headed Walter snuggled under his father's chin, and Charles found a hand to spare for both Mamey and Katey. Beside them Charley beamed from his mother's lap.

"We've been away far too long, Kate," Charles said.

That summer they all went to the seashore at Broadstairs. The white spaniel, Timber Doodle (shortened to Timber) went along, too. There they remained until September, while Charles worked each morning at *American Notes*. Every day he looked out the window at his children. His eyes rested especially upon Charley "digging up the sand on the shore with a small spade, and compressing it into a perfectly impossible wheelbarrow. The cliffs being high and the sea pretty cold, he looks a mere dot in creation."

When his parents had returned from America, the little boy had been thrown into convulsions from sheer joy at their homecoming, and the doctor had had to be summoned. The child soon recovered. Watching the four playing in the sand, Charles felt a sense of deep thankfulness.

In October, Henry Wadsworth Longfellow made his

promised visit to England and Devonshire Terrace. Boz extended hospitality as only Boz could do. There was a round of dinners and excursions, and a trip through the London slums.

After Longfellow had gone, Charles and three of his friends—John Forster, Daniel Maclise and Clarkson Stanfield, better known as "Stanny"—went on a trip to Cornwall. For three happy weeks they cast all care aside and conducted themselves like schoolboys on a holiday. It was a time they would never forget.

The household at Devonshire Terrace was especially happy just now because Georgina Hogarth, Kate's fifteen-year-old sister, had come to live with them. The children were overjoyed. They had become deeply attached to their young aunt while their parents were in America.

For Charles the situation carried both pain and pleasure. Mary Hogarth had been about her age when she joined the Dickens household. Georgina resembled Mary so much that when the three of them sat together after the children had gone to bed, he was often carried back in time, scarcely distinguishing past from present. One thing was certain, although Charles was unaware of it. Not even Mary had adored him more.

Meanwhile *American Notes* was not getting a good reception at home or in the United States. Today one wonders why. It was good reporting. Charles praised what he liked and criticized what he disliked. In each case, he presented ample evidence. That was the way he had always written for England, and he was actually less harsh in writing of America than he had been in writing of his own country. Then, too, he had penned an introductory chapter in which he thanked his American friends for leaving him freedom to speak out as he wished; but Forster thought the words sounded apologetic and talked him out of them. Only two years after Boz's death did his readers learn of his original intentions when the chapter was included in Forster's biography of Dickens.

By now Charles was deep in his new novel, *Martin Chuzzlewit.* Coming out in installments, as all his novels did, it sold poorly at first. The author remedied matters by sending his hero to America in the fifth number. That move brought some increase in sales, but still did not completely restore Chapman and Hall's confidence in him.

Charles must have had his anxious moments, for the family at Devonshire Terrace was an expensive one. And Charles himself had lavish tastes, which he indulged freely. Yet deep within him was that iron will which in early youth had made him determined to live within his means. That resolution he never broke, although it meant long hours of unceasing labor at his desk.

But no matter how hard Charles worked, he always took time to live. His children, when they were grown, remembered their bedtime sessions with him in the rocking chair he had brought back from America. With all four of them in his lap or hanging on in some manner, he would rock violently while he sang comic songs, accompanied by their childish giggles. They would come in loudly on the chorus: "Oh, oh, oh, ri fol de riddy oddy bow wow." And the watching Timber would join in on the last two syllables.

In January, 1843, there was a Twelfth Night party to celebrate Charley's sixth birthday. It was a gala affair, with Dickens and other "children of larger growth" taking a prominent part. Aided by a friend, Charles himself became a conjurer, to the delight of his own children and their young friends.

But the question of money kept pressing at his heels. He continued to work at *Martin Chuzzlewit,* which was still disappointing in sales. As usual, the family went to Broadstairs for the summer, and of course Charles carried his work with him.

During this year he found time to advise Miss Angela Coutts, his heiress friend, with her plans for the Ragged Schools. At a time and in a country where free public education was unknown, this volunteer arrangement was an attempt to educate children whose lives otherwise would have been hopeless. Charles was thoroughly in favor of the movement. No matter how busy he might be, he always had time for any appeal on behalf of neglected children.

Although he was still writing *Martin Chuzzlewit,* October found him deep in the preparation of a little volume to be called *A Christmas Carol.* It exerted a strange fascination over him, and he completed it in late November. Although he expected the book to solve some of his financial problems, for once he did not display his excellent business sense. He himself was paying the costs of publication, and he demanded a beautiful little clothbound volume with gilt edges, colored papers, a title page printed in blue and red, and four hand-colored plates by John Leech. All this in spite of the fact that it would be sold for only five shillings.

Christmas, 1844, was a mad round of parties in the true Dickensian manner. At a children's party at the Macready home, with Macready himself on tour in America, Charles acted as a magician, having been thoroughly coached by a real one. To the delight of the children, he produced a plum pudding from an empty saucepan, kindled a blazing fire in a friend's hat without damaging it, and changed a box of bran into a live guinea pig that ran between the young guests' feet.

A Christmas Carol took England by storm. The first day's sales were six thousand copies. Letters of congratulations poured in, and the author's spirits soared. He told himself that he could expect a clear thousand pounds profit from

Salon, Palazzo Peschiere, the Dickens home in Genoa in 1844

the sale of the little Christmas book. Heaven knows he needed it, he thought. He had borrowed to meet unpaid bills, and in December he had overdrawn at his bank.

On February 10, 1844, a letter from Chapman and Hall arrived in the post. It was the long-awaited account of *A Christmas Carol*. He opened the envelope prepared to feast his eyes upon its contents. Here was the news that would quiet his fears, the magic wand that would restore him to prosperity.

Merciful fathers! The total was 230 pounds instead of the expected one thousand. Charles dropped the letter to the floor in his despair.

He was not solaced when Chapman and Hall reminded him that the cost of printing—according to his own planning—had run up the expenses of production until little profit was possible. For him this was the end. He would break relations with them as soon as possible, and that would not be soon enough.

"Bradbury and Evans have been trying to get me to come with them for some time," he told Kate grimly. "Little do they know that they will soon have me, now that the abominable letter regarding *A Christmas Carol* has arrived from Chapman and Hall. I shall proceed cautiously, of course. Forster will handle the arrangements."

"Oh, dear," Kate said helplessly. "Do you think you should?"

"I know I should," he told her. "My mind is made up. Then I shall carry out the plans that have been simmering in my mind for months. My friend Lady Blessington says that living costs in Italy are cheaper by far than in England. Tomorrow I shall put our house in the hands of agents. In June we shall go to Italy for a year. People who travel on the Continent assure me that we can live for a fraction there of what it costs in England. Angus Fletcher—you remember him—is already in Italy, and he will see to renting us a house. No doubt—"

Kate began to cry violently, and Charles paused. "Whatever in the world is wrong?" he asked.

"The children—" Kate gasped. "They are so young—I can't leave them again."

"Who said anything about leaving them?" Charles inquired indignantly. "We shall take them all with us. And Anne. And Timber. Even the raven Grip, if he wants to go."

Kate hastily dried her tears. She would have preferred to remain safe and secure at Devonshire Terrace, but she did not give the matter a second thought. When her brilliant young husband decided on a course of action, he never swerved to right or left, but drove ahead relentlessly to the carrying out of his plans.

Now that he had come to a decision, Charles was aglow with enthusiasm. Dear old Forster—the only living soul to whom he had ever confided the agony and humiliation of the blacking-factory days and the only one to whom he ever would confide it—Forster handled the details of the break with Chapman and Hall. Also he tied up the new agreement with Bradbury and Evans to Charles's satisfaction. Charles reflected with pleasure that now his former publishers would realize the sort of man they had lost. Why, they had only been unimportant printers until Boz's works had placed them among the leading London publishers!

As the days went by and June approached, Charles hit upon the plan of purchasing a coach to transport himself and his family across Europe. It would take quite a conveyance, for he listed the "caravan" in a letter to a friend:

(1) The inimitable Boz
(2) The other half ditto
(3) The sister of ditto ditto

(4) Four babies, ranging from two years and a half to seven and a half

(5) Three women servants commanded by Anne of Broadstairs

Baby Frank would be left with his Hogarth grandparents.

Charles found a coach and described it in a letter to his friend Forster: "—let me see—it is about the size of your library; with night-lamps and day-lamps and pockets and imperials and leathern cellars and the most extraordinary contrivances."

It had been marked at sixty pounds, but the bargain-driving Dickens bought it for forty-five pounds. Also he engaged the services of a French courier, Louis Roche, who was to become a friend as well.

On July 2 the passengers boarded the secondhand traveling coach, the courier cracked his whip, the horses broke into a trot, and they rolled away. At the last moment they had decided to include the baby. Kate was unwilling to be separated from even one of her children a second time. And of course there was Timber, yipping and yapping himself hoarse, in the center of everything.

TALIAN INTERLUDE

The Dickens party wended its way across France and down to Marseilles. All ninety-six bells on the collars of the four horses jingled every step of the way. At Marseilles the coach was put aboard a steamer, and the party sailed across the Mediterranean to Genoa.

Two miles beyond Genoa they came to their journey's end at the Villa Bella Vista—the House of the Beautiful View. It was a dismal-looking, shabby, deserted place, and their spirits fell when they looked at it. Charles called it the Pink Jail. But he had rented the place, sight unseen, for three months, so the family moved in and endured their stay.

For the children the long, curving Mediterranean coastline was another Broadstairs and therefore Paradise. But for the grownups it was another story. In the middle of the day they drew the blinds to shut out the heat of the sun. At night they closed the windows to shut out the mosquitoes. In addition, there were plagues of rats (battled by scores of lean cats), lizards, scorpions, beetles, frogs and, worst of all, fleas. Because of the fleas, poor Timber had most of his hair clipped off. In spite of that, he never left off scratching.

Boz adapted himself to conditions and was soon leading a lazy, happy life. He learned to speak Italian and explored Genoa, which he did not think much of. In August his paper, inkstand and the little gewgaws that he kept on his writing table arrived, but still he did not begin to write in earnest, although a Christmas story was beginning to form in his mind. With his children he enjoyed the marionette theater in Genoa where the marionettes were life-size. Then, in September, his brother Fred came for a two-week holiday.

After their visitor went back to England, the Dickens family moved to Genoa and the Palazzo Peschiere—the Palace of the Fishponds. The rent was much cheaper and the surroundings far nicer.

Set in formal gardens, the stately house looked out on seven fountains where goldfish swam in the pools under the eyes of classic sculptured figures. Groves of orange and lemon trees, through which the blue Mediterranean was visible, added to the beauty of the surroundings.

Charles was having a difficult time with his Christmas story. There were too many distractions. Then he heard that the new governor expected the famous English author to attend his levee.

Through the English consul, Charles begged to be excused because he was writing a book. When the Governor's reply arrived, Charles was touched by his kindness.

"Let no gentleman call upon Signor Dickens till he is understood to be disengaged," the Governor said.

Now Charles should have been able to begin his Christmas story, but something was wrong. Missing the crowded streets and the roar of London's traffic, he could not write. He was accustomed to taking long walks in London while his imagination was at work.

And the bells! The bells of Genoa rang without ceasing, or so it seemed to him. They awakened him from his sleep, they clanged at noon and midnight, they told the hours, the half hours and even the quarter hours. He sometimes felt they were driving him mad.

Then one day, in the midst of their ringing, there came to his mind some words of Shakespeare's Falstaff: "We have heard the chimes at midnight, Master Shallow!"

There was his title—*The Chimes!*

From that time on, he had clear sailing. He would write a story that would be "a great blow for the poor." Trotty Veck, a poor old London porter, would talk with goblins and Christmas spirits in his dreams. The laws of England would change. Charity and mercy would rule. The almshouses would be emptied, the world made over. Charles worked furiously. He began his day with a cold bath, set to work at a madman's pace, and did not stop until late afternoon. His cheeks became sunken, his hair lank and his eyes abnormally large. At last, on the third of November, he threw down his pen. He had finished *The Chimes.*

That night, when the family was gathered in the great dining room decorated with brightly colored frescoes,

Charles ate with gusto. Over dessert, he looked around at the others and announced his plans. Kate was at the foot of the table with Georgina on one side and their guest, Susan Atkins, Macready's sister-in-law from England, on the other. The children had long since been sent to bed, for the Dickens adults dined late.

Charles tossed a luscious grape into his mouth and looked benevolently about him.

"My Christmas story is done," he announced with satisfaction. "The last *t* is crossed, the last *i* dotted, my pen laid aside."

His hearers made little congratulatory sounds. Having done this, Kate went on eating a rich pastry that was bad for her figure, and Susan Atkins took on that half-sick look which she fondly imagined a young female should direct toward a successful author. Charles could scarcely keep the disgust from his face. No wonder Kate and Georgina were becoming worn out with her. But they must not show their feelings. After all, her brother-in-law, Charles's good friend, had taken the Dickens children into his home during their parents' stay in America.

Charles stole a glance at Georgina, who looked so lovely and self-possessed. She reminded him so much of Mary—but Mary was gone, and he must not allow himself to be caught up in the past.

"Now I can carry out my plans," he told his dinner companions briskly. "I have written Forster that I shall be in London by the third of December to read *The Chimes* to a select group of friends."

Kate gave a little cry. "How can we travel in such wretched weather with the children?"

"Be quiet, Kate," Georgina said quickly. "He doesn't mean us."

He threw her a grateful look. Kate assumed a pouting

Sydney Smith Haldimand Dickens

Charles Culliford Boz Dickens at fifteen

Edward Bulwer Lytton Dickens ("Plorn")

Henry Fielding and Francis Jeffrey
Dickens

Walter Landor Dickens

Mary Dickens ("Mamey")

Kate Macready Dickens (Mrs. Perugini)

expression, and Susan continued to look soulful. Charles uttered a silent thanks that he would soon be far away from the Palazzo. Let Georgina cope with her sister and their guest. She was quite capable.

He thrust a feeling of guilt into the background and went on. "I shall take Roche with me to see to the luggage and the other details of traveling. Of course we shall use a public conveyance instead of the great old family coach. After a quick trip to England, I will have a glorious reunion with my friends, and we will be back in Genoa for Christmas. What do you say to that?"

It was a cold, wet day in November when Charles and Roche set out. At first they made slow progress over the muddy roads in the unceasing rain, but the weather improved as they went along. Parma, Ferrara, Venice and Milan lay ahead. Boz jotted down his impressions, for the form of his *Italian Sketches* was already beginning to take shape in his mind. Soon the travelers would cross the Channel and then—London!

Charles spent eight splendid days there with every hour filled to the fullest. At first the final revision of his manuscript and conferences with his publishers occupied every minute.

Then it was the third of December. Forster had promised to gather a special audience for Charles's reading. At the appointed time, a group of about ten friends assembled in his rooms at Lincoln's Inn Fields to listen to the Goblin Story. The dour Thomas Carlyle was there, and so was Clarkson Stanfield. It was a most satisfactory gathering.

The artist Maclise sketched the scene that night with rays of light surrounding Boz's head, but he could not sketch the spirit of close association that bound the group together.

It was an age of social reform, and all over England people were beginning to look to Dickens to be their spokesman. In *The Chimes* he spoke out boldly against a society that set the rich against the poor—the haves against the have-nots. The story has a strangely modern ring.

Altogether, it was a great night. The guests were unrestrained in their enthusiasm, and Charles warmed himself in the glow of their approval.

After the reunion with his friends, he hurried back to Italy, pausing only for a three-day stay in Paris with Macready, who was playing Shakespearean roles there. Boz felt he *must* be with his family for Christmas. All his life holidays, birthdays and similar occasions meant much to him. Pushing through snow and slush, he managed to reach Genoa in plenty of time.

Christmas was a great affair, but in the Dickens family it was always overshadowed by Twelfth Night and Charley's birthday. This time the party was truly magnificent, for Miss Coutts in London had sent her godchild a cake weighing ninety pounds. It was a splendiferous affair decorated with bonbons, crackers and Twelfth Night characters. Nothing like it had ever been seen before in Genoa, or so they said at the pastry cook's, where it was sent to repair damages suffered on the journey. As for the party, to which the children in the English colony were invited, it was noisy enough and hilarious enough to satisfy even Charles.

After a few more months in Italy, the Dickens family packed up once more. In June of 1845 the old coach was loaded up again. The baggage that could not be carried with them was sent on in another conveyance. Charles and the faithful Roche climbed up on the box, the horses headed northward and the party was on its way.

Over the Alps in Switzerland—down to the lowlands—on to Brussels—and at last, after a whole year's absence, home in London once more!

The family soon settled down at 1 Devonshire Terrace. *The Chimes* had sold well. Charles's earnings from books still controlled by Chapman and Hall were encouraging. He was out of debt and beginning to build up a surplus. And, best of all, he was back in England. Life looked very bright indeed.

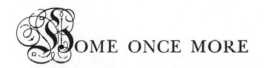

HOME ONCE MORE

As soon as Charles returned from Italy, he joyfully pushed
to completion a plan that had been born during his brief
trip to London just before Christmas. He began work on the
casting and production of Ben Jonson's *Every Man in His
Humour*. For the cast he collected his friends and acquaintances, including John Forster. He also enlisted his
brothers Fred and Augustus.

Charles directed the rehearsals. At the same time he was

Dickens as Captain Bobadil in Every Man in His Humour

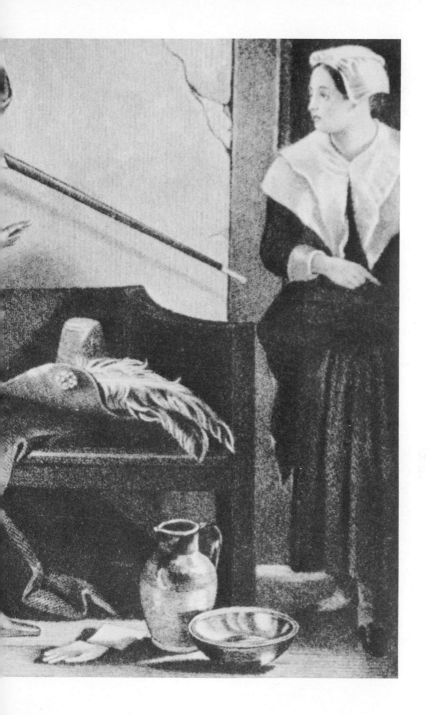

carpenter, property man, prompter and musical director. And that was not all. In the cast he was the braggart Bobadil, gotten up in boots, spurs and black beard.

The performance was so successful that the actors agreed to a repeat performance. This time it was attended by many members of the nobility and Prince Albert himself.

On October 28, 1845, Kate gave birth to another child— their sixth—whom the parents named Alfred Tennyson.

With a constantly growing family, it is small wonder that Charles was always aware that he must bring in an increasing income. He was sure he could become an actor if his popularity as a writer waned. And another idea had been growing in his mind for months. As a young man he had been a journalist. Now, he would found a newspaper.

When Charles Dickens made plans, people usually listened. His new publishers, Bradbury and Evans, were no exception. They accepted his ideas for a liberal newspaper to be set up in opposition to the conservative London *Times*. There were evils to be fought—corruption in high places, inefficiency, the deplorable condition of the masses. They were clarion calls to the reformer in Boz.

Backers were quickly found all over England. Charles assembled his staff. He demanded and was promised an annual salary of two thousand pounds instead of the thousand he had first asked. Preparations for the launching of the paper went on with breakneck speed.

On January 21, 1846, the first issue of the *Daily News* came off the press. Charles felt that his rival, the *Times,* had purposely attacked his recent Christmas book, *The Cricket on the Hearth.* He was doubly glad when the first issue of the *Daily News* had a good sale.

But something happened. The old restlessness increased. He was surrounded by unfinished writing and his promises to write more. His bills were mounting again. His health was none too good. And time and again he would take up his pen only to stare at the blank paper for hours. The old ability to write anywhere at any time had deserted him.

No doubt all this made him irritable. At any rate, he quarreled with Bradbury and Evans, and after eighteen stormy days resigned as editor of the *Daily News*. He persuaded the faithful John Forster to take his place. It must be remembered that Charles Dickens instituted a newspaper that today publishes more than a million copies a day.

Soon Charles and his family were on the move again. Once more they leased Devonshire Terrace. Once more he hired Roche as courier. Wherever they stopped at inns, heads were turned to look at the party of two ladies, six children, four servants and a little dog, all under the direction of Charles Dickens, aged thirty-four.

Their destination was Lausanne, Switzerland. There they rented a sort of doll's house called Rosemont, which overlooked Lake Leman and the Castle of Chillon. Charley was put in school and the rest of the family settled into their regular routine.

Seated at a window overlooking mountain gorges whose sides rose up to the Simplon Pass, Charles at last began his new book, *Dombey and Son*. Writing it was not easy. He missed the sounds of the London streets, the weather was hot and muggy and he had to fight the flies.

"They cover everything eatable, fall into everything drinkable, stagger into the wet ink of newly-written words and make tracks on the writing paper, clog their legs in the lather on your chin while you are shaving in the morning, and drive you frantic at any time there is daylight if you fall asleep," he said.

Charles would be the last to admit that his furious drive was slowing up a bit, but it was true.

Catherine Dickens in 1846 (painted by Daniel Maclise)

At last *Dombey and Son* got under way. The writing became easier as he went along. He read the first installment to friends at Lausanne, who praised it highly. Encouraged, he had a sudden idea. Why, in months to come, should he not give readings from his books? It would undoubtedly bring in considerable money. He tucked the thought away in his mind for future reference.

With difficulty he undertook the writing of his Christmas book. He would call it *The Battle of Life*. Although he did not enjoy writing it, he finished it in October, three weeks before he set out with the family for Paris.

He arrived there in November with "tons of luggage, other tons of servants, and other tons of children." He rented a house in the Rue de Courcelles which, he wrote his friend Forster, was a cross between a "babyhouse," a haunted castle and a mad kind of clock. The premises belonged to a Marquis Castellane, and Forster was promised that he would be ready to die of laughing when he visited them.

In the midst of his writing, Charles found time to dash over to London, confer with his publishers, and take over the direction of *The Battle of Life*, which was to be presented on the stage during the Christmas season.

Shortly after his return to Paris, Forster came over for a two-week visit. When the guest went back to England, he was to be accompanied by ten-year-old Charley, who was to be enrolled at Eton. His godmother, Miss Angela Coutts, would pay for his schooling.

When the time came for Charley to leave, his father went along to see him off at the railroad station. The little boy looked pale and forlorn in the midst of the surging crowds and thundering trains.

"I don't want to go, Papa," he said in a small voice.

Charles felt a wave of sympathy for the child. He looked as lonely as that boy of long ago who had wandered about London after his working hours at the blacking factory.

"You mustn't say that, Charley," his father chided gently. "What would Miss Coutts think? This is a great opportunity."

His son did not reply. He only bit his lip while his eyes brimmed with tears.

John Forster threw a comforting arm about the thin little shoulders. "Charley and I will do all right. Never fear. He will be a proper young Etonian when you see him next."

Charles stood looking after them as they climbed aboard the train. The last glimpse he had of his son was a small white face pressed to the train window and a little hand waving farewell.

The man on the platform was filled with grief as the train pulled away. "I didn't know it would be so hard," he mourned. "I didn't know."

Two weeks later a message came that Charley was ill of scarlet fever at the home of his Hogarth grandparents. In those days it was a dreaded disease. Charles left the other children with Georgina in Paris while he and Kate hurried across the Channel to London. The child was quarantined, and it was days before the anxious father was allowed to see him.

When Charles stood at last by his son's bedside, he realized how much The Phenomenon—he still thought of him by that name sometimes—meant to him.

"We're here in London to stay," he told the pale little patient.

"You're not going back to Paris?" Charley asked unbelievingly.

His father shook his head. "I've taken a house in Chester Place until we can get our own dear home back. Your Aunt Georgina will bring the other children over soon, and then we will be one big happy family again. You will stay at home until you are stronger."

The Dickenses soon had another addition. Born in April of 1847, he was named Sydney Smith Haldimand; he was more often called Speck. His father insisted that on their holiday at Broadstairs that summer the infant stared out to sea like an Ocean Spectre. The summer vacation at the shore was marked by a brief visit from Hans Christian Andersen, whose fairy tales were "special favorites" of Boz. The two men were together only a few hours, but they parted the best of friends. They would not renew the visit for ten years.

The year 1848 brought more than its share of sadness. Some months earlier Charles had learned that his beloved sister Fan was suffering from tuberculosis. In those days one seldom recovered from the disease. Charles did all he could, but there was little anyone could do. Henry Burnett, Fanny's husband, was not a wealthy man, but he had enough to make her comfortable.

Charles was with his sister toward the end. In this white, spent woman coughing her life away, it was hard to see the Fan he had known so well. Yet the ghost of her old laughter was there, and he marveled at it.

"Look after my little Harry, Tom Thumb," she begged. "His father will miss me so at first that the child may feel very much alone—and he isn't strong."

"I will, Fan," Charles promised. The thought of his crippled nephew made the moment even more painful.

"You and I used to have such good times together. Remember?"

A spell of coughing cut her words short, and Charles, holding her hand, remembered. He remembered the parties at Chatham in those early days when he was not aware of that important thing called money. He remembered her at the Academy of Music when he, a shabby, threadbare boy, had called to accompany her to the Marshalsea. He remembered her, bright and gay, in the Furnival's Inn days when she and Henry Burnett, like Kate and himself, were happy and young.

Little Henry Burnett did not survive his mother long. He died early in 1849, but Boz kept his memory green as Paul Dombey in *Dombey and Son,* which he concluded in March, 1848.

Charles Dickens did little writing in 1848, but that little made literary history. *The Haunted Man* was his Christmas contribution. In January, 1849, Kate had her eighth child —"what the Persian Princes might have called a 'moon-faced' monster," as Charles put it. They named him Henry Fielding Dickens. In due time he became the grandfather of the modern English novelist, Monica Dickens.

Soon after the birth of Henry Fielding Dickens, Charles began to consider the story that became *David Copperfield.* He loved the book—his "favorite child" and so much his own story. The writing of it came hard at first, as writing always did after his early years, but once he got into *David Copperfield* he wrote with rapidity and ease. David and Little Em'ly and Peggotty and the wicked Murdstones and all the rest of those enchanting characters will live forever.

When Dickens was writing this book, not even a change of scenery affected him. He wrote at home, he wrote on the Isle of Wight where he took the family for the summer, he wrote at Broadstairs, and still his ideas flowed. He had not felt so contented and so well in years. In November, 1850, he would write the last words of his *magnum opus*—his masterpiece.

Meanwhile he had been busy in another field of endeavor as well. When New Year's Day had ushered in 1850, he was deep in plans for founding a monthly magazine. The first issue was dated March 30, 1850, but he had been at work on it long before that. *Household Words* would be a modern magazine portraying "social wonders, good and evil, in the stirring world about us." Although the editorship of the *Daily News* had been a distasteful thing to him, the same post on the new magazine seemed much easier to fill. He called himself "conductor," not editor. He took care to own half the stock. With Forster owning a one-eighth interest, Dickens virtually had control of *Household Words*.

In the summer of 1850 the Dickenses' ninth child, a girl, was born. They called her Dora—for David's Dora in *David Copperfield*, who was really Maria, the lost love of Charles's youth.

Household Words had caught on at once. Charles had hit his stride, journalistically speaking. He had found a place where he belonged.

AVISTOCK HOUSE

Not even an editor's chair could separate Charles Dickens from the world of the theater. In late 1850 he was deeply involved in private theatricals at Knebworth, the country estate of Edward Bulwer-Lytton.

Dickens and Bulwer-Lytton had been friends, after a fashion, for more than ten years. The tall, handsome dandy —one of a group of several like himself—had been Charles's model in the early days when he was first coming into public view. The young author had copied his dress, jewelry and long, curling hair from the popular novelist, who was nine years his senior.

The friendship, while not an intimate one, had flourished, and now Charles was overjoyed at the opportunity of being an actor in the "Dramatic Festival" to be held at Knebworth. The medieval mansion was crowded with "Dukes, Duchesses and the like" for three nights during November. A great number of Bulwer-Lytton's friends and neighbors in Hertfordshire came in their carriages to be a part of the audience.

The festival proved to be the beginning of the Guild of Literature and Art, an undertaking dear to Charles's heart. While the project did not work out as time went on, its spirit of seeking to aid young actors and reward older ones was noble in intent.

In March, 1851, old John Dickens died. He had been ill for some time, but had hidden his pain from his family. When Charles was notified of his father's grave condition, he hastened to his bedside. There he soon forgot what a trial the older man had been, and remembered only how a man and a boy had gone on long walks together; how the father had taken pride in displaying his son in songs and recitations; how he had been gentle and kind and loving, with a zest for life equaled only by that of Charles himself.

Fate was shortly to deal him a worse blow than his father's death. Little Dora Annie, not yet a year old, had been ill earlier in the winter, but seemed to have made a complete recovery. Now she became suddenly ill again and died while her father was at a public dinner and her mother away from home for her health.

After the funeral, Charles rented a house in Broadstairs. They would not return to Devonshire Terrace. It was too full of memories of little Dora. The twelve-year lease would be up in September; it was time to look for another house.

The family remained at Broadstairs during the summer of 1851 while Charles went back and forth between London and the seashore. Even then he had time to go on a boating trip with Charley and three of his Eton friends. None of the four boys ever forgot the long row down the river, the prodigious lunch and the royal tea at a public house on the homeward journey.

But there were not many holidays for Charles. When his duties kept him in London, he spent his nights on an iron bed set up in his office at the headquarters of *Household Words*. When he could spare time from his editorial work, he spent it house-hunting. The search came to an end when he found Tavistock House, a four-story mansion looking out on a park. More spacious than Devonshire Terrace, it had ample room for his many children and for frequent entertaining. It would be a place for Charley to bring his friends from Eton. Besides, Mamey and Katey would soon be young ladies. And he himself, as a prominent author, had a position to maintain.

Tavistock House was in bad repair, but Charles's love of order rectified that. As usual, he visited the shops and planned the furnishings. By now he felt he had become an expert on the subject of curtains and carpets, not to mention furniture.

He used an unusual device in the library to preserve appearances. He ordered dummy book-backs to bridge the shelves on the door opening between his study and the drawing room. The general effect was an unbroken line of volumes.

Charles chuckled as he stood with his hands behind him and surveyed the titles. *"Cat's Lives,* in nine volumes," he said with a grin, *"Swallows on Emigration, Lady Godiva on the Horse, Cockatoo on Perch, Noah's Arkitecture.* That took cleverness, my good man, real cleverness."

By the last of November the family had moved in, and Boz was settled in his study. He was ready to begin *Bleak House.* His favorite objects—the dueling green-bronze frogs, the man with puppies wriggling out of his pockets, the ivory paper knife—were ranged on the desk, along with a plentiful supply of paper, ink and pens. Before Christmas he had made a good start on the new novel.

Of course there was the usual Twelfth Night party in 1852, with the Dickens children (directed by Charles) presenting the burletta *Guy Fawkes.* There was dancing afterward for the children and their guests, with their Aunt Georgina valiantly attempting to keep the girls supplied with partners. Watching them, Charles sighed. They were so young, so fresh, so *shining.*

Charley was home from Eton with a fuzz on his upper lip. Mamey was nearly fourteen now—a quiet, retiring child. Katey was twelve and continued to live up to her nickname of Lucifer Box. Charles recognized Annie and Minnie Thackeray in the crowd of young guests. Their father was there, too. Charles was never quite sure whether to regard the man as a friend or a rival—or both. Nevertheless, he liked Thackeray.

The party was a magnificent affair, and Tavistock House afforded a fitting background for it. After the guests had departed, leaving behind the usual after-party mess, Charles reflected with satisfaction that his children would never need to find the world as hard as he had found it when he was young.

He looked with some distaste at the disorder of chairs, the rolled-up carpets, the confusion of plates, cups, spoons and napkins on the banquet tables.

"All this must be shipshape before breakfast in the morning," he told Georgina. "I can't endure untidiness."

She laughed and made him a mocking bow. He smiled as he turned away, but they both knew that his wish would be obeyed.

The first installment of *Bleak House*, which came in March, 1852, had a great reception. That same month Kate had a baby boy—Edward Bulwer-Lytton Dickens. He was their tenth and last child.

Success had come, but the years were marching on. Several of his friends had died, and Charles noted that he himself felt tired and overworked. "The spring does not seem to fly back again directly as it always did," he remarked.

The summer of 1853 found him with his family at Boulogne. There at the end of August he finished *Bleak House* —an attack on the chancery courts of England, where wills and the settlements of estates dragged out a weary course. This book proved at first to be even more popular than *David Copperfield*.

Sending the family home to London—except for Alfred and Frank, who were left in a private school in France— Charles started on a two-month tour of Europe with two friends. On the return he had a short visit with Charley, who met him in Paris. The son, having decided against a profession, had left Eton and decided on a mercantile career. He was studying German in Leipzig and at sixteen had grown out of his clothes at such a rate that his father bought him a new outfit.

Charles soon hurried home to be with his family for Christmas. Upon his arrival he threw himself into plans for a Twelfth Night play, which again, of course, he directed. Before the sixth of January arrived, he gave three readings at Birmingham for that city's newly established Institute.

Tavistock House, Dickens' home from 1851 to 1860, where he wrote Bleak House *and* Little Dorrit

These marked the beginning of his public readings, which he had been considering for a long time.

He presented *A Christmas Carol* on December 27, *The Cricket on the Hearth* on December 29, and a second reading of *A Christmas Carol* on December 30. Each time the audience ranged in size from 2,000 to 2,500 people, and they gave him applause such as he had not dreamed of. He had begun a practice that would last as long as he lived.

The year 1854 had hardly begun before Bradbury and Evans called a conference. Financially *Household Words* was not faring well. Its circulation was slipping. Something must be done.

Since *The Child's History of England* had been brought to a conclusion in December, the publishers suggested that Charles could improve matters by contributing a new serial to the magazine. Charles was more than willing. For some time a story about the evils of England's industrial system had been brewing in his mind. Thus it was that *Hard Times* came into being. He worked at it with all his heart, finishing it in Boulogne where the family had gone again for the summer.

In mid-1854, as Charles brought *Hard Times* to an end, he was in a pessimistic frame of mind. His health may have been partly to blame. Finishing a novel in six months had drained him to the point of exhaustion. But the cause went deeper than that. There were so many problems to be attacked: education, slum clearance, sanitation, hours and wages, factory and mining conditions. Any efforts that had been made to solve these issues had been dropped at the onset of the Crimean War, which was still going on.

The old restlessness had increased, and Charles was well aware of it. "If I couldn't walk fast and far, I should just explode and perish," he complained to Forster.

Why did he feel like this, he wondered. What more could

a man ask for than he had? Wealth, position, fame, a loving family were his. Yet something was lacking.

In February, 1855, he learned that Gad's Hill Place, which as a child he had dreamed of owning, was for sale. He attempted to buy it, but his plans fell through.

With this disappointment there were renewed within his heart memories of past happy times when he had been young and ambitious and longed to be "a learned and distinguished man." Now that he had reached that state, he found that life was not so bright as he had imagined it would be.

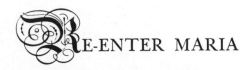

RE-ENTER MARIA

Charles was going to Paris with his friend Wilkie Collins. Owning to the illness of the subeditor at *Household Words,* Boz had been doing double duty there. Too, he felt exhausted from writing *Hard Times,* and he was growing no younger. He had turned forty-three a few days ago. He needed to rest and he knew it, but something within him continued to drive him on.

To Forster, who urged him to slow down, he had said: "I

am the wrong man to say it to. I have now no relief but in action. I am incapable of rest. I am quite confident I should rust, break, and die, if I spared myself. Much better to die, doing. What I am in that way, nature made me first, and my way of life has, alas! confirmed."

But for a few brief moments he was about to find time suspended—or better still, turned back to the days of his first love.

It happened in this manner. He was to leave the next day for Paris. The prospect of the trip was not bringing him as much pleasure as he had hoped, although he knew he would have a brief visit with his sons Alfred and Frank, who were at school in Boulogne.

On Saturday night he sat turning over the letters which a servant had just brought in and laid on the table. He knew only too well what they would contain. An invitation to a testimonial dinner for someone almost a stranger. A plea to use his name for some charity. A bill from his tailor or his wine merchant.

He was about to toss them back in a pile when the handwriting on one caught his eye. Although it had a familiar look, for a moment he was puzzled. Then he knew. His hands trembled as he tore open the square white envelope. He turned quickly to the signature, but there was no need. Only one person in the world had that handwriting: Maria.

The years dropped away like magic. Charles was seventeen once more . . . or was it eighteen? He knew only in his middle-aged heart that he was miraculously young again. He looked out at the slushy London streets and saw only April and violets—and Maria.

He sat down at once to write her. He addressed the envelope to Mrs. Henry Louis Winter, but he poured out his heart to Maria Beadnell. Not a faded, aging Maria but the girl he had adored in his youth.

"Three or four and twenty years vanished like a dream, and I opened it [her letter] with the touch of my young friend David Copperfield when he was in love," he wrote her.

Charles could not believe that Maria had two little girls "until it occurred to me that perhaps I had nine children of my own!"

Maria wrote that she read his books with interest, as had half of England, but that only when she came to Dora Spenlow and her little dog Jip in *David Copperfield* had she recognized herself and the long-departed Daphne. (Later when Charles visited Maria, he found Daphne, stuffed, in a glass case in the entrance hall. The Victorians had a way of preserving their pets with the help of the taxidermists. One of the Grips—Dickens had two ravens by that name—looked down from his niche on visitors to Tavistock House.)

Maria's letter must have touched off a string of recollections, for Charles in his letter to her reminisced about the house on Lombard Street that had seemed so grand to him, the harp she had played "like an angel," and even the little blue gloves he had been commissioned to match for her. Carried away by thoughts of himself as a very young man he forgot he was writing to a woman his own age. In fact, because he always projected himself so thoroughly into his own characters, he became the young David Copperfield writing to Dora, the object of his dreams.

There was a note of sadness, too, in his letter. "We are all sailing away to the sea," he said, "and have a pleasure in thinking of the river we are upon, when it was very narrow and little."

In spite of what the years had taught him about human nature, he forgot—if he had ever admitted it—that the Maria he had known was shallow, flirtatious and thoughtless. He saw only the ideal built up by a boy with stars in his eyes.

In his letter he told her that he was going to Paris the next morning, but that he would see her when he returned. In the meantime, he assured her that his wife would call upon her with an invitation to dinner, and that the Dickenses and the Winters would spend a quiet evening together.

Kate made the call, and when Charles returned from Paris, the couples met for dinner. In fact, from letters still existing it is clear that Charles was careful to meet Maria before the dinner.

The balloon was punctured. She had warned him that she was "old, fat, and ugly," but he had not believed her. Nothing has been written about what she herself saw, but the slightly balding, weary man with beard and moustache was certainly not the romantic, pink-cheeked youth who had danced attendance upon her some twenty-five years ago.

As for her, the middle-aged matron had kept her girlish ways. She walked, giggled and rolled her eyes as though she were a girl of seventeen. It was, Charles thought, as though one tried to recall to life an old play "when the stage was dusty, when the scenery was faded, when the beautiful actors were dead, when the orchestra was empty, when the lights went out."

When the two couples finally met for dinner, Maria committed the unpardonable sin of giving Charles her cold, which was accompanied by a bad case of sniffles. His emotions cooled off rapidly. In fact, they had been extinguished when he first set eyes on her after a quarter of a century.

Maria would appear in yet another novel of his. Flora in *Little Dorrit* is a take-off on the mature Maria. It is extremely doubtful that she ever recognized herself. To Maria, a primrose by the river's brim was just a yellow primrose—nothing more. As a girl and as a woman she simply could not recognize the fire, the imagination, the ecstasy that

Mrs. Henry Louis Winter (Maria Beadnell in later life)

marked Charles Dickens. It is not surprising that she and Charles's prosaic wife became good friends—they had much in common.

If Charles seems to have been a little cruel in portraying Maria Winter as Flora, it must be remembered that Flora, for all her faults, was kind and gentle. Certainly the youthful Maria had been heartless in her treatment of an adoring boy. Could such a shallow girl have grown into a woman like Flora? It is doubtful; yet that is just how Dickens depicted Flora in *Little Dorrit*.

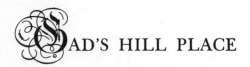# GAD'S HILL PLACE

Gad's Hill was his at last. He found it hard to believe even when he was deep in consultation with carpenters and painters and other workmen. At first he had no thought of living there but only of using it now and then. Between times he would lease it.

The roots of his possession dated back to a summer day in 1855 when he had walked with his friend William Henry Wills, the subeditor of *Household Words,* past the old rose-brick dwelling on the Dover Road.

"There it is," Charles said. "It seems a hundred years ago that I walked here as a small boy with my father. He told me, I remember, that if I would work very hard and save my money, I would someday own the place."

The younger man looked at him with compassion. The lines in Boz's face had deepened with the years. The bright-blue eyes had taken on an expression of sadness which made him appear older than forty-three. Charles Dickens was a famous man, but he was not a happy man.

The electric-blue eyes suddenly twinkled, and a decade dropped away from him. "Heaven knows I have worked hard, Wills, but I have not saved my money. Perhaps that is why the Governor's promise hasn't come true. But nine children—"

The next day, an excited Wills approached his superior. "I have great news, sir," he announced. "Last night at dinner I sat next to one of our contributors, Mrs. Lynn Linton. I mentioned that I had been in the neighborhood of Gad's Hill that day."

"Don't tell me that she wants it, too," Charles returned with an amused smile.

"She owns it!" Wills shouted. "She grew up there. She has just inherited it from her rector-father's estate, and it is on the market. I tell you, sir, that it is written you were to have that house at Gad's Hill."

Thus Charles came into his own. The purchase was made final on March 14, 1856. Seventeen hundred pounds was paid over, with an extra ninety pounds for the shrubbery across the road. That seemed a bit unusual, but Mrs. Linton would have it no other way. And what is ninety pounds for the realization of a dream?

Although the present resident of the house would live there for another year, Charles was soon in a maze of ditch-diggers, bricklayers and the like, for he was making

Dickens in 1856

the alterations necessary for the installation of a large family. In early 1857 he took rooms at a hotel in Gravesend, where he could come over to Gad's Hill every day to oversee operations.

By his hurrying along the workers, the house, which had undergone extensive changes, was ready for occupancy by June 1, 1857. Accordingly the family moved in for the summer. Charles continued to keep Tavistock House for a town residence.

The first guest at Gad's Hill was Hans Christian Andersen, who came for two weeks and remained five. The younger Dickens children—Sydney, Harry and Edward, or Plorn, as they called him—thought him delightful. They were enchanted by the dancing elves and fairies he could cut from a folded square of paper. A tall, awkward man, he played in the hay and strolled in the meadow with them as though he were their age.

But Mamey and Katey considered him a "bony bore," and as time passed, Charles agreed with his daughters. To Miss Coutts he wrote that they were "suffering a good deal from Andersen."

At last the Dane said his farewell, unaware that he had worn out his welcome. To this day there is a card tucked in the corner of the dressing-table mirror in the bedroom that he occupied. On it Charles Dickens wrote: "Hans Christian Andersen slept in this room for five weeks which seemed to the family ages."

A few days after Andersen's departure, Charles and his eldest son accompanied Walter, the sixteen-year-old, to the ship that was to bear him away to India. Miss Coutts, who had seen Charley established with a brokers' firm in London, had obtained a cadetship with the East India Company for Walter.

The parting hurt his father more than it hurt the boy.

Charles and the older brother inspected the tight little cabin that would be his home for some time to come. The young cadet had stowed away his belongings, including the case containing quinine, essence of ginger, opium and other medicines provided by the company for their men going out to the Orient.

Charles turned away abruptly. Another bird was leaving the nest. Before long he found himself on the dock returning the wave of the smartly dressed young fellow in uniform and shako who stood on the upper deck of the departing ship.

Charles turned to the son at his side. "It's like having great teeth drawn with a wrench," he said disconsolately. "Your brother seems in good spirits. Heaven be thanked for that. I myself have said so many goodbys that I wonder if man could not be defined as a parting and farewell-taking animal."

It was indeed a farewell. A few years later Walter fell victim to India's climate. He died on the last day of the year 1863.

After the summer was over, the family returned from Gad's Hill to London. There were still repairs and changes to be made, and Dickens was not a wealthy man. He was a successful author-editor-actor who must keep producing if the money was to continue rolling in.

He gave a benefit reading of *A Christmas Carol* for the Children's Hospital in London. Its success was tremendous. Against the advice of Forster—who was proved wrong—Charles now undertook a tour of the British Isles with his readings. Mamey and Katey joined him to go to Scotland and witness the applause and praise heaped on their father. The money poured in for his many expenses—family, needy relatives, living expenses and the beautification of the new home.

Dickens reading to daughters Mamey and Katey, circa 1865

Before summer came again and Charles Dickens and his family came back to Gad's Hill, England was shocked by the news that he and his wife had separated. Now people began to understand the consuming restlessness that had urged their beloved Boz on at such a pace for years. At times financial difficulties may have contributed to that restlessness, but the real reason behind it was the "incompatibility of mind and spirit" that existed between Catherine and him. He could find no peace when peace did not exist at home.

Much has been written about the separation. Some people have sympathized with Dickens, some have criticized him. The truth is simply that the two persons could no longer live together.

Kate agreed to live in a house provided by Charles with an income of six thousand pounds a year. The children were free to come and go as they pleased. Charley, at his father's request, would live with his mother.

The children suffered, as was inevitable. "Nothing could surpass the misery and unhappiness of our home," Katey said.

Poor Charley, torn in two directions, told his father, "Don't suppose that in making my choice, I was activated by any preference for my mother to you. God knows I love you dearly, and it will be a hard day for me when I have to part from you and the girls."

Walter was in India; Sydney had joined his brothers, Alfred and Frank, at their French school. That left Henry Fielding (Harry), aged nine, and Edward Bulwer-Lytton (Plorn), aged six, at home with Mamey and Katey, who were twenty and nineteen respectively. And Georgina was there to look after everyone, including Charles.

Upon his return to London, Charles immediately broke off relations with his publishers, Bradbury and Evans. At the height of the uproar about the separation, he had been furious with them for refusing to print a statement from him in the pages of *Punch*. Now he decided to go back to Chapman and Hall. Hall was dead, but Chapman welcomed him.

Resigning from the editorship of *Household Words*, Charles purchased the magazine when it was sold at auction in March, 1859. At once he started a magazine of his own called *All the Year Round*. He insured the success of the new magazine by writing for its pages *A Tale of Two Cities*.

In 1860 Katey married a man whom her father felt she did not love. Perhaps her marriage was a means of escaping a bad home situation. For, despite the fact that she adored her father, Katey felt her mother had been badly treated, and defiantly paid visits to her. In contrast, Mamey did not see her mother until after Dickens's death.

When Katey's wedding was over and the guests had departed for London, Mamey missed her father and went in search of him. She found him on his knees beside Katey's bed with his face buried in her wedding gown.

"But for me," he wept, "Katey would not have left home."

After Katey's marriage her father sold Tavistock House and moved all his possessions that did not go with it to Gad's Hill. By now he had brightened the front of the old house with beds of scarlet geraniums and built a tunnel under the Dover Road to his land on the other side.

Now he began *Great Expectations* for *All the Year Round*. The magazine's sales shot up and continued to rise. When *Great Expectations* went into book form, it reached a fourth edition in a few weeks. Dickens was still the Inimitable Boz.

But his personal problems were increasing. Frank, who had been put to work in the office of *All the Year Round*, was proving inefficient. Alfred was not succeeding in the

Royal Military Academy. Plorn, who was at Wimbledon with Harry, was not doing well in his studies.

When Charley married Bessie Evans, the daughter of Frederick Evans, of Bradbury and Evans, Dickens did not attend the wedding. His reason was twofold: Both his estranged wife and the publisher with whom he had quarreled would be there. But the next Christmas found Charley, Bessie and their baby girl at Gad's Hill. With some of his old spirit, Dickens exclaimed, "Think of the unmitigated nonsense of an inimitable grandfather!"

Meanwhile, the readings went on. They weakened him, they drained him—and they were the breath of life to him. He was as sensitive to audience reaction as the small boy at Chatham had been when his father swung him up on a table to sing to the guests.

His current book was *Our Mutual Friend,* in twenty issues for *All the Year Round.* When he was not on tour with his readings, he was writing. At Gad's Hill he now had a new and pleasant place in which to write. An admirer had sent him a gift in fifty-eight boxes. When they were opened, they proved to be the parts of a small Swiss chalet, made to fit together like the pieces of a puzzle.

Charles had it erected among the trees of the shrubbery across the road from Gad's Hill Place. There he spent happy hours at work, away from the house, where people were always coming and going.

Although he wanted time to work, he loved people around him. The day at Gad's Hill began with breakfast served from nine to ten-thirty. The guests coming down the stairs from their bedrooms saw a plaque on the first-floor landing:

This House, GAD'S HILL PLACE, stands on the summit of Shakespeare's Gad's Hill, ever memorable for its association with Sir

John Falstaff in his noble fancy. *But, my lads, my lads, tomorrow morning, by four o'clock, early at Gad's Hill! there are pilgrims going to Canterbury, with rich offerings and traders riding to London with fat purses; I have vizards for you all; you have horses for yourselves.*

Beyond the square entrance hall the downstairs stretched pleasantly away to include a dining room, bright with mirrors, where Dickens played the cordial host. After breakfast he went off to his writing, while his guests entertained themselves, reading, strolling about the grounds or conversing.

The host loved to show the visitors about the little estate, from the horses in their stables to the watchdogs chained at the entrance gate. Then there were the walks. A twelve-mile walk in three hours was routine for him, even though physically he was not the man he once was. And after walks there were games of battledore, bagatelle, bowling, quoits. When dinner was over, there was dancing. The guests sometimes went to bed exhausted, but Charles was the last to retire.

Yet he was forced to admit, more times than he cared to, that he was bone-tired. The will to do was there, but physically he was exhausted.

MERICA AGAIN

In 1866 the Messrs. Chappell of Bond Street became the managers of Charles Dickens's readings. It was an arrangement that proved to be more than satisfactory. They appointed George Dolby as his advance agent and personal representative. He removed a mountain of work from Charles's shoulders.

"All I have to do is take in my book and read it at the appointed place and hour," Boz said.

Under the new firm's direction the readings, which had been discontinued for some time, were resumed. They were still a drain upon Charles's health, and he was far from well. His doctor had told him that his heart was involved, and that he must slow down. He went ahead with the readings, anyway. When he had set upon a course of action, nothing could stop him.

There was no change in the author-actor's preparations, except that now Dolby made them. Every detail was carefully attended to. At the appointed moment, Charles would come on stage—usually limping, for a leg had given him trouble for months. Greeted by vociferous applause, he would carry the audience with him into the magic world of his own creation.

Soon America was urging Dickens to make another visit. The sting of his *American Notes* had apparently been forgotten.

A group of gentlemen in Boston offered to deposit a guarantee of ten thousand pounds in a London bank. That settled the matter; Charles was not mercenary, but money was necessary for his way of life. He was a generous man, and his greatest wish was to leave his children in comfortable circumstances. He was sure the proceeds of this trip would do it.

His friends urged him not to go because of the state of his health. He listened to their objections and then followed his own inclinations. To Georgina and his daughter Mary he explained:

"I began to feel myself drawn toward America as Darnay in the *Tale of Two Cities* was attracted to the Loadstone Rock, Paris . . ."

Landing in Boston on November 19, 1867, he was met by Dolby, who had come earlier to make arrangements. As before, a large group of editors and reporters was there also. Dolby took him to his suite on the third floor of the Parker House, where he was gratified to learn that the advance ticket line had been almost half a mile long. Every ticket had been sold and $14,000 taken in. Already speculators were selling $2 tickets for $26.

The readings were spaced to allow Charles time to renew old friendships and to rest his left foot, which was no better than it had been for the last six weeks in England. The hours passed pleasantly with visits from Longfellow, Emerson, Holmes, the zoologist Agassiz, and other Bostonians.

Boston turned out in record crowds to listen to him read *A Christmas Carol* and *Bardell vs. Pickwick*. Before he moved on to New York, he found that the four Boston readings had netted more than $9,000.

In New York, history repeated itself. The ticket line numbered five thousand people. In the Mercantile Library, where there had been nineteen hundred volumes of his works, only two had not been borrowed. That week he sent home $3,000.

For Christmas he swung back to Boston, where he was entertained by a charming hostess, Mrs. James T. Fields. From there he went again to New York. Now his route included Philadelphia, Baltimore and Washington. During the second half of his stay in America he visited towns in New England, going as far north as Portland, Maine.

There was hardly a day when he did not wish himself home with his dear ones, for his health did not improve. Influenza, which he had contracted upon his arrival in America, had left him with a heavy cough that he was unable to get rid of.

Dolby, who proved a friend as well as a manager, appointed himself nurse and fed Charles egg-and-sherry at frequent intervals when he was able to take nothing else.

"The Empty Chair" painted by Sir Luke Fildes

The leg continued to give trouble, and the strain of the readings often left him in a frightening condition, with his blood pressure soaring.

Yet when Charles Dickens mounted the rostrum, the audience forgot the aging man before them. From the first word he held them spellbound. In his readings he was not an actor; he was many actors. He became his characters. With no properties, change of costume, or scenery, he could conjure up one enchanting character after another. In years to come, one of Longfellow's daughters, who, at twelve was taken to a reading, would recall:

Sam Weller and Mr. Pickwick, Nicholas Nickleby and the old gentleman and the vegetable marrows over the garden wall. How he did make Aunt Betsy Trotwood snap out, "Janet, donkeys"—and David Copperfield yearn over the handsome sleeping Steerforth. How the audience loved best of all the Christmas Carol and how they laughed as Dickens fairly smacked his lips as there came the "smell like an eating house and a pastry cook's next door to each other, with a laundress's next door to that," as Mrs. Cratchit bore in the Christmas pudding and how they nearly wept as Tiny Tim cried, "God bless us everyone!"

One of the most charming accounts of his visit is *A Child's Journey with Dickens,* written by the author and educator, Kate Douglas Wiggin.

As a child she was with her mother on a train bound for Boston when she recognized her idol, whose pictures were everywhere during his American tour. When Charles's companion left for the smoking car, she lost no time in taking his place in the seat beside Boz.

"God bless my soul, where did you come from?" the Great Man exclaimed.

"I came from Hollis, Maine," she stammered, "and I am going to Charlestown to visit my uncle. My mother and her cousin went to your reading last night, but, of course, three couldn't go from the same family, so I stayed at home . . . There was a lady who had never heard of Betsy Trotwood, and had only read two of your books!"

"Well, upon my word!" he said. "You do not mean to say that you have read them!"

"Of course I have," she replied, "every one of them but the two that we are going to buy in Boston, and some of them six times . . . Of course I do skip some of the very dull parts once in a while . . ."

He laughed heartily. "I distinctly want to know more about those very dull parts."

Out came his notebook and pencil while he questioned her about the books with the dull parts.

"What book of mine do you like best?" Dickens asked the child.

"Oh, I like *David Copperfield* much the best. That is the one I have read six times."

"Six times—good, good!" he replied. "I am glad that you like Davy, so do I—I like it best, too!"

As the enchanted hour on the train went on, he asked, "Did you want to go to my reading very much?"

The child could hardly answer. She faltered, "Yes, more than tongue can tell."

She looked up and to her astonishment saw tears in his eyes to match those in her own.

"Do you cry when you read out loud?" she asked. "We all do in our family. And we never read about Tiny Tim or about Steerforth when his body is washed up on the beach, on Saturday nights, or our eyes are too swollen to go to Sunday School."

"Yes, I cry when I read about Steerforth," he answered quietly.

The train was approaching Boston and the passengers

were collecting their wraps and bundles. Several times Dickens's traveling companion had come back, but had been waved away by Boz.

"You are not traveling alone?" he asked.

"Oh, no," the little girl answered sweetly. "I had a mother, but I forgot all about her."

Dickens smiled. "You are a past mistress of the art of flattery."

In spite of pain and bad health, Charles concluded his tour on a triumphant note. Only a few days before he sailed for home, he made a speech in New York in which he thanked the people of America for their generosity and magnanimity. In closing, he said:

The English heart is stirred by the fluttering of those Stars and Stripes, as it is stirred by no other flag that flies except its own. I do believe that from the great majority of honest minds on both sides, there cannot be absent the conviction that it would be better for this globe to be riven by an earthquake, fired by a comet, overrun by an iceberg, and abandoned by the Arctic fox and bear, than that it should present the spectacle of these two great nations, each of which has, in its own way and hour, striven so hard and so successfully for freedom, ever again being arrayed the one against the other.

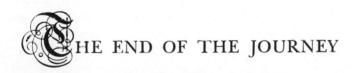

HE END OF THE JOURNEY

Charles was a sick man when he sailed away from the shores of America in the spring of 1868. But a few days of inactivity at sea—and the knowledge that he was carrying home a net profit of nearly twenty thousand pounds—seemed to make a new person of him. His doctor in England upon seeing him exclaimed: "Good Lord! seven years younger!"

Now that he was back in England he should have followed a lighter schedule, or no schedule at all, but the word *rest* was not in Charles's vocabulary. His welcome at Gad's Hill Place and the surrounding countryside was tumultuous. Even the dogs—Don, Bumble, Linda, Mrs. Bouncer—were beside themselves. The houses on the homeward route from the train station were draped with flags; as for Gad's Hill, "every brick of it was covered." Even on Sunday, after the morning service in the little church Dickens attended, the bell ringers rushed out and rang the bells madly to celebrate his return.

The work he must do had piled up. His subeditor on *All the Year Round,* having suffered a hunting accident, was out of the picture. The finances of the magazine had been completely in his hands, and Dickens now was forced to learn that aspect of the business from the beginning.

He was not too busy in June, 1868, to play host to Longfellow and his three daughters when they came to England and visited Gad's Hill. In the best tradition, they were driven about on the old royal Dover Road in a chaise drawn by four horses and manned by two red-coated postilions. Dickens himself no longer drove—"for fear of a momentary seizure," he confided to a friend, although he refused to acknowledge the seriousness of certain symptoms he had developed.

As for family matters, Charles's sons continued to be problems. Harry alone was doing well at school and preparing for Cambridge, but his father found the costs staggering.

In addition, Dickens was outfitting Plorn, the youngest son, to go out to Australia and join Alfred, who had sailed for that country in 1865. Charley, whose paper business had just gone bankrupt, he took into the office of *All the Year Round,* in the hope that his firstborn might find himself there.

Dickens in 1868

Nave of Rochester Cathedral, a childhood haunt of Dickens

It was clear that, for a time at least, the readings must go on. If money was to go out, then it must come in from some source. There seemed no quicker and more satisfactory way than the readings.

In December Charles began them again. After each performance he was utterly exhausted. His friends pleaded with him to discontinue the program, but he ignored them until his doctor intervened. Even then he chose to taper off the readings rather than stop them at once. The toll upon his health was what might have been expected. By the time he reluctantly abandoned them, his health had gone farther downhill than ever before.

And so Charles came home to Gad's Hill, but he did not stay there. He went back and forth to London. He accepted invitations to dinners and invitations to speak. He even accepted an invitation to Buckingham Palace for an audience with the Queen. He limped to the office of *All the Year Round* nearly every day. His leg was steadily growing worse.

The theater still delighted him. When friends in London were producing some private plays in which his "girls," Mamey and Katey, were acting, he rehearsed the company daily and intended to take a part, but his lameness would not allow that. However, he worked as stage manager and prompter until the production was over.

In May, 1869, he welcomed American friends to England. They were Mr. and Mrs. James T. Fields. He had known the Boston publisher and his wife ever since his first visit to the United States, and they were his close friends. Other travelers from America were with the Fields party. In order to be with them in London, Charles engaged a suite at the St. James Hotel, in Piccadilly, for himself, Mary and Georgina. He was the Americans' guide in London from the darkest haunts of the slums to Windsor Castle.

Of course Gad's Hill and Rochester were not neglected. Again the chaise with four horses and the red-coated postilions was brought out. The party was treated to the sights of Kent and Canterbury while Charles pointed out the scenes he had loved since boyhood. It would be his last journey to the Cathedral, although neither he nor his guests knew it then. At the end of the day the gates of Gad's Hill Place opened invitingly to receive them.

During their visit, an idea for a novel was forming in his mind. It had come to him in the depths of the London slums when he was escorting Fields and his friends there. He would call it *The Mystery of Edwin Drood* and, for the most part, it would be laid against a background of the ancient Canterbury Cathedral.

The American party returned to London and Charles continued his strenuous mode of living. The months passed, and Christmas he spent at Gad's Hill with that part of his family still in England. Harry was doing well at Cambridge. His father felt that his son was on the way to becoming a successful lawyer.

Early in January, 1870, Charles resumed his readings in spite of the wishes of his children and the family doctor. His performances proved as popular as ever, but with each appearance his blood pressure rose alarmingly. He could hardly make his way backstage to the sofa where he lay exhausted. Even he knew that the readings must stop.

At the last performance, an audience of two thousand gave him a thunderous ovation. He could not speak, for he knew this marked for him the final curtain. When he found his voice, he concluded: "From these garish lights I now vanish forevermore, with a heartfelt, grateful, respectful, affectionate farewell."

Once more they called him back. He kissed his hand to

The Swiss Chalet, in which Dickens wrote the last lines of Edwin Drood

them and limped off the stage. The lights dimmed, the curtain fell. That part of his life was ended.

During his lifetime he had given more than four hundred readings. He estimated that he had cleared some 45,000 pounds. This was nearly half the value of his estate when he died. The little blacking-factory boy had achieved success, but the achieving had shortened his life by many years.

It was June when he returned to Gad's Hill to stay. The country was filled with the beauty of early summer, and he took keen delight in the peace of the old house he loved. Katey paid a short visit, and although the father and the daughter sometimes had their differences, they seemed to grow closer together and gain a fresh understanding of each other during these days. When she returned to London, Mamey soon followed for a visit with her.

On June 8, 1870, Charles worked all day in the chalet across the road on *The Mystery of Edwin Drood*. The last words he wrote described the Canterbury Cathedral, which had always exercised such a peculiar fascination over him:

Changes of glorious light from moving boughs, songs of birds, scents from gardens, woods, and fields—or, rather, from the one great garden of the whole cultivated island in its yielding time —penetrate the Cathedral, subdue its earthy odour, and preach of the Resurrection and the Life. The cold stone tombs of centuries ago grow warm; and flecks of brightness dart into the sternest marble corners of the buildings, fluttering there like wings!

In the evening he returned to the house, where he and Georgina were to dine alone. At dinner he fell to the floor, unconscious. Doctors were summoned, his children were sent for, but there was nothing to be done. The house that had resounded so many times with laughter and lively con-

*Westminster Abbey, the Poet's Corner. Dickens' grave is at
lower right.*

versation and music was very still as Charles Dickens drew his last breath.

Long ago, in *Domby and Son,* he had written:

The golden ripple on the wall came back again, and nothing else stirred in the room. The old, old fashioned! The fashion that came in with our first garments, and will last unchanged until our race has run its course, and the wide firmament is rolled up like a scroll. The old, old fashion—Death!

He had made it clear in his will that he desired a private funeral, and the family carried out his wishes. He had said also that he would like to rest in the graveyard beside the little church where Katey was married. But that was not to be. Charles Dickens lies today in the Poets' Corner, in Westminster Abbey.

He died nearly a hundred years ago, and yet he is not really dead. Every generation discovers him for itself. In this decade Broadway has presented *Oliver Twist* and *Pickwick Papers* as musical comedies, a form he surely would have loved. What a pity he could not have been there to direct them! His books, written for the most part against a nineteenth-century background, are as fresh as though they had just come off the press. David Copperfield, Nicholas Nickleby, Sydney Carton, Little Nell, Florence Dombey, and a host of other characters are as dear to those of us who love them as are our friends of flesh and blood.

Of each book which Charles Dickens wrote, a true Dickensian can say, in the words of an earlier Englishman: "It is a tale which holdeth children from play, and old men from the chimney-corner."

BIBLIOGRAPHY

BECKER, MAY LAMBERTON. *Introducing Charles Dickens.* New York: Dodd, Mead & Company, 1940.

CHESTERTON, G. K. *Charles Dickens.* New York: Dodd, Mead & Company, 1907.

JEANS, SAMUEL. *Charles Dickens.* London: A. & C. Black, Ltd., 1929.

JOHNSON, EDGAR. *Charles Dickens: His Tragedy and Triumph.* Boston: Little, Brown and Company, 1952.

JOHNSON, EDGAR. *The Dickens Theatrical Reader.* Boston: Little, Brown and Company, 1964.

JOHNSON, EDGAR. *The Heart of Charles Dickens.* New York: Duell, Sloan and Pearce, 1952.

PEARSON, HESKETH. *Dickens: His Character, Comedy, and Career.* New York: Harper & Row, 1949.

POPE-HENNESSEY, UNA. *Charles Dickens.* New York: Howell, Soskin, Publishers, Inc., 1946.

NDEX

A

B

Baltimore, 106
Barnaby Rudge, 95, 97, 98
Barrow, John Henry, 57
Battle of Life, 133
Bayham Street, 28
Beadnell, Anne, 45, 48
Beadnell, Margaret, 48
Beadnell, Maria (Mrs. Henry Lewis Winter), 45-55, 71, 95, 137, 147-151
Beadnell, Mr., 54
Beadnell, Mrs., 46, 50, 51, 54
Beard, Tom, 58, 72
Beetham, Arthur, 48
Bentley, Richard, 77, 95
Bentley's *Miscellany,* 77, 95
"Blue-Eyed Maid", 26
Boston, 104, 107, 108, 163, 164
"Boz", 63
Bradbury and Evans, 117, 130, 131, 158, 160
Braham, 77
Britannia, 101, 104
British Press, 42
Broadstairs, 139, 140
Brook, The, 24
Browne, Hablot Knight, 75, 76, 86-89
Bulwer-Lytton, Edward, 138, 139
Burdette-Coutts, Miss Angela, 85, 114, 125, 133, 155
Burnett, Henry, 80, 136
Burnett, Henry (son), 136
Buss, Robert William, 75

C

Camden Town, 33, 36, 38
Chalk, 73
Chandos Street, 39
Chapman and Hall, 61, 67, 85, 90, 100, 113, 117, 126, 159

N

O

P

R

S

ABOUT THE AUTHOR

Katharine E. Wilkie has read and loved the novels of Charles Dickens for as long as she can remember. In this biography for young people, she takes readers through the fifty-eight years of his remarkable, and often tragic, life. "I think I know him so well," she writes, "that I would recognize him if I met him on the street or if he rang my front door bell."

Mrs. Wilkie is the author of 17 books, mostly in the field of biography for children and young people. She teaches high school English in the Kentucky school system, in addition to her writing, and manages to do both with talent and enthusiasm. She and her husband have two sons.